AN EVERYDAY
BOOK OF HOURS

AN EVERYDAY
BOOK OF HOURS

A FOUR-WEEK CYCLE
OF MORNING AND EVENING PRAYER

WILLIAM G. STOREY

LTP

LITURGY
TRAINING
PUBLICATIONS

ACKNOWLEDGMENTS

We are grateful to the many publishers and authors who have given permission to include their work. Every effort has been made to determine the ownership of all texts and to make proper arrangements for their use. We will gladly correct in future editions any oversight or error that is brought to our attention.

Many of the prayers in this book are translations by the author of old Latin texts; some are original compositions. Many antiphons, verses and responses are adaptations of scripture by the author, as is the Canticle of the Three Youths on pp. 26–27, 35–36 and 44–45. It is adapted from Daniel 3:52–57 which appears in The Prayer of Azariah: 29–35 in Bibles that treat this material as noncanonical.

Acknowledgments continued on page 295.

AN EVERYDAY BOOK OF HOURS © 2001 Archdiocese of Chicago: Liturgy Training Publications, 3943 South Racine Avenue, Chicago IL 60609; 1-800-933-1800; fax 1-800-933-7094; orders@ltp.org; www.LTP.org. All rights reserved.

Visit our Web site at www.LTP.org.

This book was edited by Lorie Simmons and Gabe Huck. Carol Mycio was the production editor. The cover design is by Larry Cope, and the typesetting was done by Jim Mellody-Pizzato in Stempel Garamond and Trajan. Printed in Canada. The interior is based on a design created by Lisa Buckley.

12 11 10 09 08   6 5 4 3 2

Library of Congress Control Number: 2001095189

ISBN 978-1-56854-278-2

EVBKHR

FOR DOROTHY DAY (1897–1980)

Friend of God and of the poor who wrote to me about the earlier edition of this book:

Your book is a joy to me. Will you call the press and order ten for me? Leaving for Pittsburgh on 9:00 AM bus today to talk at the Merton Center and mention your book as a tremendous aid to prayer. My talk will be on the primacy of the spiritual. Too many social workers today. We must pray unceasingly and your book goes along. A good meditation day on the bus, 9:00 AM–5:00 PM. Peace, quiet and joy.

TABLE OF CONTENTS

Introduction to An Everyday Book of Hours   viii

First Week   2

Second Week   65

Third Week   129

Fourth Week   194

Night Prayer   257

Appendix

   Biblical Readings throughout the Liturgical Year   268
   Hymns for Morning and Evening Prayer   272
   Basic Prayers   285

Introduction to An Everyday Book of Hours

MORNING AND EVENING PRAYER IN THE CATHOLIC TRADITION

Several foundation stones of Christianity have their origins in Judaism: the seven-day week with one day kept as a holy day, daily prayer services at set times, and the use of the psalms and other biblical poetry in worship. Other essential principles developed in early Christian communities: the celebration of the paschal mystery each week and the use of New Testament texts in prayer.

Like the Jews, early Christians opened and closed the day with prayer, both privately and in community. They did this on the Lord's Day and on weekdays. As Christianity assumed official status in the Roman Empire of the fourth century and church buildings appeared, bishops instituted morning and evening prayer in their cathedral churches. Parish churches also adopted this practice so that, very literally, it became the prayer of the entire church. The daily schedule for prayer, called the "daily office," came to include additional times, but morning and evening prayer (lauds and vespers) remained the pivotal hours.

Eventually the daily office became burdened with far too many psalms and with devotional items, but most early cathedral offices were short—one or a few psalms—with a large element of intercessory prayer, usually litanies. Their primary component was songs drawn from holy scripture: psalms and canticles from the Old and New Testaments.

Jesus and the apostles, like all Jews of their time, would have prayed the psalms throughout their lives, and the New Testament writers often portray them speaking in the words of the Hebrew psalmist and prophets. Those writers, and the early Christian teachers who came after them, heard the Book of Psalms as the poetic masterpiece of the Bible. Baptized into life in Christ, these Christians saw all of scripture in the light of Christ. That perspective continues to influence the way we hear and pray the psalms today.

Jews have always read the psalms differently; their encounter with God in those songs is as stimulating and nourishing a spiritual mystery to them as our meditations on Christ are to us. We honor their experience and would be enriched by understanding it better.

Our Christian perspective on the psalms has provided a rich formation for praying the Liturgy of the Hours. Thomas Merton, in *Bread in the Wilderness,* spoke eloquently about the Christian lens through which we read the psalms and why the church in its liturgy has always turned to them for sustenance: "The psalms acquire, for those who know how to enter into them, a surprising depth, a marvelous and inexhaustible actuality. They are bread, miraculously provided by Christ, to feed those who have followed him into the wilderness. . . . The reality which nourishes us in the psalms is the same reality which nourishes us in the eucharist, though in a far different form. In either case, we are fed by the Word of God."

Today's Christians may find it hard to recognize in the psalms and canticles the mystical power that Merton speaks of and that captivated the founders of the liturgy. But the daily office helps us sense the Christian insights in these ancient texts. By praying them in the context of refrains, prayers and other scripture readings, we come to know in them the complete Christ of the past and the present in his head and members.

Daily prayer is a school where we learn, progressively and deeply, the complete divine plan of salvation as it stretches from the distant past through the present into the future. Reflecting on the Savior's role in all of the inspired poetry of the Bible is a venerable practice. Saint Luke shows us the risen Christ teaching it to Cleopas and his wife on their way to Emmaus: "Beginning with Moses and all the prophets, he interpreted to them the things about himself in all the scriptures." And not only did Jesus do this for them, but the same passage reveals to us what happens to believers when Christ speaks in the liturgy now: Jesus had "vanished from their sight. They said to each other, 'Were not our hearts burning within us while he was talking with us on the road, while he was opening the scriptures to us?'" (Luke 24:27, 32).

In the first half of the twentieth century, after a long period of dissatisfaction with the older form of the office (the Roman Breviary), numerous teams of biblical scholars and liturgists prepared for the renewal of the hours of prayer. Thanks to their historical research and pastoral efforts, the Second Vatican Council proposed the restoration of the Liturgy of the Hours—and particularly morning and evening prayer—to families, religious communities and churches. The Council also encouraged individuals to immerse themselves in this ancient form of scriptural prayer. So far, this vision has been only partially fulfilled in the official Liturgy of the Hours.

THIS BOOK OF HOURS

This book of hours builds on the sound foundations just described by presenting a four-week cycle of psalms and canticles for morning and evening that complement one another. They are placed in a setting of Bible verses and prayers designed to bring out a fuller sense of all the scripture. Each week highlights the mystery of Christ's dying and rising—keeping Friday as the day of his passion and death, and on Sunday celebrating his glorious resurrection, the gift of the Spirit, and his coming again in glory to judge the living and the dead.

Each hour has the same structure:

- opening verses

- an optional hymn

- a psalm with antiphon, silent prayer and a psalm prayer

- a short reading from scripture with silence and a verse response

- a canticle, usually from the Bible

- intercessions (in the evening)

- the Lord's Prayer followed by a concluding prayer

- a final blessing

This prayer book is designed for personal or communal use in or outside the home. Its elements come from our many-layered Catholic tradition and can be adapted to seasons and to the varying needs of individuals and small groups. Families and other groups may find it works best to gather for this common prayer either just before or after meals. Although this book can be used year-round, some may wish to pray the hours more thoroughly in tune with the seasons by using a related publication: *A Seasonal Book of Hours.*

HOW TO PRAY THIS BOOK

ABOUT BEGINNING

An Everyday Book of Hours provides four weeks of morning and evening prayer. Because the church begins its celebration of Sunday on the previous evening, each week starts with Saturday evening.

Four-week cycles are now the church's pattern in the Liturgy of the Hours. This is *your* four-week cycle. You begin whenever you wish and simply repeat the cycle after you've completed the four weeks.

FOLLOWING THE SCRIPT

For each morning and evening within the four-week cycle, you will find a kind of "script" for prayer. In the opening verses of the script a small cross [+] reminds you to sign your lips with this traditional gesture as you begin the hour. The same cross will appear in the closing verses when you sign your entire body.

Most of the texts are given in the script, but a few are not. The hymn, a traditional element in morning and evening prayer, is optional. It may be chosen from those located on pages 272–284. Two familiar pieces of worship, the Lord's Prayer and the Apostles' Creed, are indicated by their titles only. Look for their full texts in the Basic Prayers section, pages 285–294.

The italicized verse after the title of the psalm or canticle is an antiphon (refrain). Taken usually from the New Testament or the psalm itself, it offers a focus point for the scripture. The antiphon is meant to be recited at least at the beginning and end of the psalm or canticle.

When more than one person prays morning or evening prayer together, a leader usually alternates speaking parts with the group. In this book the symbol [~] has been used to indicate the group's response to the leader's part—in opening verses, responses to the readings, intercessions, psalm prayer and closing blessings. When praying the psalm prayer the leader customarily begins by saying, "Let us pray" and then pauses to allow time for the group's silent prayer before reciting the prayer text.

Intercessions have two patterns in this book. In litany intercessions in which the same response (such as "Lord, hear our prayer") is given to each intercession, the leader's invitation, "Let us pray to the Lord," has been indicated after the first intercession only. However, leaders would include it after each. Since the response is consistent, spontaneous intercessions from the group can easily be added. Spontaneity is more difficult for the second pattern of intercession, which calls for a different response to each intercession. But groups and individuals should make the modifications that will serve them best.

ALLELUIAS AND OTHER SEASONAL MATTERS

This book is designed to stand alone throughout the year, so you are invited to make small modifications appropriate to the seasons of Advent, Christmas, Lent and Easter. During Lent the church abstains from "Alleluia," and you may wish to leave out that eastery exclamation of joy when you encounter it on Sundays during the season of Lent. The following canticles, placed on Saturday Evenings or Sunday Mornings, are really most appropriate outside of Lent: Canticle of the Lamb's Wedding (First Week, Saturday Evening), Canticle of the Church (First and Third Week, Sunday Morning) and Canticle of Christ our Passover (Second and Fourth Week, Saturday Evening). During Lent replace these with any of the canticles on Fridays.

As you get to know this pattern of prayer and become familiar with the resources in the Appendix, you may adjust elements to suit the season or feast.

It is well to remember that what counts in prayer is quality rather than quantity. A few prayers said with attention and devotion are far more valuable than many with a wandering heart and mind. Sincerity and attention to meaning are the essence of prayer.

THE TEXTS IN THIS BOOK

Traditionally, scripture readings for the Liturgy of the Hours come mainly from the Old Testament and epistles. Outside of the Canticles of Zachary and of Mary (sometimes called the *Benedictus* and the *Magnificat*), the gospels appear only in brief phrases in the antiphons and responses. But this book presents a wider variety of texts. Canticles and scripture readings are drawn from all parts of the Bible, and a few Catholic classics outside of scripture also serve as canticles. Many of the intercessions and other prayers have been gathered from throughout the Christian tradition; a number of texts were composed or translated by the author. In the psalms when the word *Lord* appears in small capitals (LORD) it represents the unutterable name for God appearing in the Hebrew text as YHWH, sometimes translated as Yahweh.

YOUR SETTING FOR MORNING AND EVENING PRAYER

Choose the most conducive space for your daily prayer. Families may wish to gather around their table, just before or after breakfast and dinner. Other small groups might arrange themselves antiphonally (facing each other), creating two parts for reciting the psalms.

Whether praying in a group or alone, you will feel more prayerful with a little attention to the environment—perhaps some sacred images or objects, a family Bible, candles. (Children love to light candles, and so do most adults.) Marking the liturgical seasons and feasts with green, purple, white, red or gold and other festive colors invites us into the sacred time of the church year.

WHEN YOU PRAY ALONE

- Before starting to say the words of morning or evening prayer, make a real effort to stand in silence before the living God who is always present in the depths of our souls. Be present to God by a loving attentiveness and by a keen desire to know, love and serve God in the here and now of our lives. Many people find a quiet, intense use of the Jesus Prayer a helpful prelude to all attempts at private and public prayer. (See Basic Prayers, page 285.)

- After the period of silent prayer, say the opening verses while making the sign of the cross on your lips.

- If you wish, sing or recite the appropriate hymn from the Hymns section at the end of the book.

- Recite the psalm aloud with attention and devotion. The antiphon is usually recited just before and just after the psalm but, for further emphasis, it may be inserted between each stanza of the psalm.

    After finishing the psalm with its antiphon, pause for a few moments to meditate on the psalm as a whole or on a verse or two. At the end of this silent prayer, say the psalm prayer that interprets and applies the psalm itself.

- Read the brief lesson from scripture, mull it over a bit, and try to see some personal application. If time permits, feel free to substitute the longer scripture passages from "Biblical Readings throughout the Liturgical Year," pages 268–271. A brief response made up of verses from scripture or the liturgy follows the lesson and leads into the canticle, a song usually taken from the Bible. On Saturday evenings and Sunday mornings after the canticle we recite the Apostles' Creed, that prayerful affirmation of faith that renews the vows of our baptism.

- Each day of worship draws to a close with prayers of petition, spontaneous or prepared, and concludes with the Lord's Prayer, the closing prayer and the blessing.

  People who pray these forms of morning and evening prayer by themselves should remember that they are never praying them alone. As full members of the whole church spread throughout the world, they belong to the communion of saints, no matter the time, the place or the circumstances. Among those praying the hours individually, it is hoped that this book will particularly benefit the old, the sick, and the homebound or bedridden. Individuals, of course, enjoy greater freedom of posture than do groups.

When You Pray in a Group

A designated leader may

- start the opening verses, making the sign of the cross on the lips at the cue [+] given in the text

- lead the singing or reciting of the hymn, if desired

- start the psalm, allow for the period of silence and then pray the psalm prayer

- start the response after the scripture reading and its silent pause

- start the canticle with its antiphon

- on Saturday evenings and Sunday mornings, start the Apostles' Creed

- lead the evening intercessions and the time of spontaneous prayer

- start the recitation or chanting of the Lord's Prayer

- pray the closing prayer and ask the blessing

- if desired, invite a sign of peace at the end of evening prayer

Designate a reader to proclaim the scripture lesson. The reading may be introduced with the phrase, "A reading from the Book of . . ." At the end of the proclamation the reader allows a pause and then concludes with, "The word of the Lord." All respond, "Thanks be to God."

GROUP RECITATION OF THE PSALMS AND CANTICLES

There are several possible ways of reciting the psalms and canticles in a group:

- The leader begins the antiphon and all join in. Then the leader recites each stanza of the psalm and all repeat the antiphon immediately after each stanza.

- The leader begins the antiphon and all join in. Then the leader alternates the stanzas of the psalm with the group. At the end of the psalm all repeat the antiphon in unison. This is the most common method.

- The leader begins the antiphon and all join in. Then the group divides in two and alternates the stanzas of the psalm between the two halves. The antiphon is repeated by all at the end of the psalm.

POSTURES AND GESTURES

Each individual or group will do what best fits its needs. Traditionally, worshipers stand for the opening verses, hymn and prayers, but sit for the psalms, readings and responses and the canticles, except for the Canticle of Zachary and the Canticle of Mary, both of which begin with the full sign of the cross. It is appropriate to stand for the Creed, for intercessions, the Lord's Prayer, closing prayer and blessing. The sign of the cross usually opens and closes the hour, and a bow is customary at the naming of the Trinity in doxologies.

SILENCES

Silence is a crucial element in the Liturgy of the Hours. During each hour there should be silence in several specific places. Before beginning, worshipers quiet themselves for prayer. After the psalm and before the psalm prayer a silent pause allows the images from the psalm to inspire silent prayer before the psalm prayer is prayed. After the reading and before the response a generous silence lets the words of scripture sink into the heart. A pause after the evening intercessions and before the Lord's Prayer gives individuals time to add their own petitions, either silently or aloud. Although space was limited in the script to signal all of these silences (only the silence after the reading is marked), prayer will be richer if readers observe them.

❀

God should be adored frequently and always.

~Saint Cyprian of Carthage, ca. 200–258

❀

SATURDAY EVENING

Light and peace **+** in Jesus Christ our Lord.
~*Thanks be to God.*

HYMN

PSALM 145:13–21

*Let me speak your praise, O Lord, for ages
unending.*

You are faithful in all your words
and loving in all your deeds.
You support all those who are falling
and raise up all who are bowed down.

The eyes of all creatures look to you
and you give them their food in due season.
You open wide your hand,
grant the desires of all who live.

You are just in all your ways
and loving in all your deeds.
You are close to all who call you,
who call on you from their hearts.

You grant the desires of those who fear you,
you hear their cry and you save them.
LORD, you protect all who love you;
but the wicked you will utterly destroy.

Let me speak your praise, O LORD,
let all peoples bless your holy name
for ever, for ages unending.

PSALM PRAYER

Gracious and merciful God,
you support the falling,
and raise those bowed down.
Be near to those who call out to you
for food, justice and freedom.
Be the Lord of the poor and forsaken
and grant them their heart's desire.
We ask this in Jesus' name.
~*Amen.*

READING   *Romans 13:11–14*

Sisters and brothers, it is now the moment for
you to wake from sleep. For salvation is nearer
to us now than when we became believers;

the night is far gone, the day is near. Let us then
lay aside the works of darkness and put on
the armor of light; let us live honorably
as in the day, not in reveling and drunkenness,
not in debauchery and licentiousness, not
in quarreling and jealousy. Instead, put on the
Lord Jesus Christ, and make no provision for
the flesh, to gratify its desires.

SILENCE

RESPONSE

Surely I am coming soon, says the Lord.
~*Amen. Come, Lord Jesus!*

CANTICLE OF THE LAMB'S WEDDING
Revelation 19:1b – 2a,6b – 8

*Blessed are those who are invited to the
marriage feast of the Lamb.*

Halleluja! Praise God!
Salvation and glory and power to our God,
for his judgments are true and just;

Halleluja! Praise God!
For the Lord our God, the Almighty reigns.
Let us rejoice and exult
and give him the glory.

Halleluja! Praise God!
For the marriage of the Lamb has come,
and his bride has made herself ready;
to her it has been granted to be clothed
with fine linen, bright and pure—
for the fine linen is the righteous deeds
   of the saints.

Glory to the Father, and to the Son,
and to the Holy Spirit:
as it was in the beginning, is now,
and will be for ever. Amen.

APOSTLES' CREED

INTERCESSIONS

Lord Jesus Christ, who died for our sins
and rose for our justification:
~*Hear us, risen Lord.*

Lord Jesus Christ, who destroyed death
by your death and gave life to those in the grave:
~*Give fresh life to a fallen world.*

Lord Jesus Christ, who established
the new and eternal covenant in your blood:
~*Unite God and humanity in true religion.*

Lord Jesus Christ, who set us free
from the law of sin and death:
~*Free us from anger, hatred and ill-will.*

Lord Jesus Christ, who stands and pleads for us
at God's right hand:
~*Save us from disease, famine and war.*

Lord Jesus Christ, the same yesterday, today
and for ever:
~*Raise us to new life in you.*

LORD'S PRAYER

Let us pray as Jesus taught us:
~*Our Father . . .*

CLOSING PRAYER

Risen Christ,
by virtue of your passing over from death to life,
pour your Holy Spirit into our hearts.
Fill us with awe and reverence for you
and love and compassion for our neighbor,
for yours is the power and the glory,
now and for ever.
~*Amen.*

May the Word made flesh, full of grace and
truth, + bless us and keep us.
~*Amen.*

O Lord, **+** open my lips.
~And my mouth shall declare your praise.

This is the day the Lord has made! Alleluia!
~Let us rejoice and be glad! Alleluia!

HYMN

PSALM 93

*Christ is victor, Christ is ruler, Christ is
Lord of all!*

The LORD is king, with majesty enrobed;
the LORD is robed with might,
and girded round with power.

The world you made firm, not to be moved;
your throne has stood firm from of old.
From all eternity, O Lord, you are.

The waters have lifted up, O LORD,
the waters have lifted up their voice,
the waters have lifted up their thunder.

Greater than the roar of mighty waters,
more glorious than the surgings of the sea,
the LORD is glorious on high.

Truly your decrees are to be trusted.
Holiness is fitting to your house,
O LORD, until the end of time.

PSALM PRAYER

Lord Jesus Christ,
reigning in glory,
by the power of your resurrection
rise with might in our hearts
and fill us with the beauty of holiness.
You live and reign for ever and ever.
~*Amen.*

READING *Colossians 3:1–4*

Brothers and sisters, if you have been raised
with Christ, seek the things that are above,
where Christ is, seated at the right hand of God.
Set your minds on things that are above, not
on things that are on earth, for you have died,
and your life is hidden with Christ in God.
When Christ who is your life is revealed, then
you also will be revealed with him in glory.

SILENCE

RESPONSE

Having been raised from the dead! Alleluia!
~*Christ will never die again! Alleluia!*

CANTICLE OF THE CHURCH

We praise you, O God,
we acclaim you as Lord;
all creation worships you,
the Father everlasting.
To you all angels, all the powers of heaven,
the cherubim and seraphim, sing in endless
    praise:

Holy, holy, holy Lord, God of power and might,
heaven and earth are full of your glory.

The glorious company of apostles praise you.
The noble fellowship of prophets praise you.
The white-robed army of martyrs praise you.
Throughout the world the holy Church
    acclaims you:

Father, of majesty unbounded,
your true and only Son, worthy of all praise,
the Holy Spirit, advocate and guide.

You, Christ, are the king of glory,
the eternal Son of the Father.
When you took our flesh to set us free
you humbly chose the Virgin's womb.
You overcame the sting of death
and opened the kingdom of heaven
    to all believers.
You are seated at God's right hand in glory.
We believe that you will come to be our judge.

Come then, Lord, and help your people,
bought with the price of your own blood,
and bring us with your saints
to glory everlasting.

APOSTLES' CREED

LORD'S PRAYER

Let us pray as Jesus taught us:
~*Our Father . . .*

CLOSING PRAYER

Father of glory,
you raised Jesus Christ from the dead
and enthroned him at your right side.
Rescue us from our sins,
raise us up with Christ,
and give us a place with him in heaven,
in the same Christ Jesus our Lord.
~*Amen.*

Peace be with the whole community, and love
with faith, from God the Father + and the
Lord Jesus Christ.
~*Amen.*

Jesus Christ + is the light of the world! Alleluia!
~*A light no darkness can extinguish! Alleluia!*

HYMN

PSALM 110

*Christ must reign until God defeats all enemies
and puts them under his feet.*

The LORD's revelation to my Master:
"Sit on my right;
your foes I will put beneath your feet."

The LORD will wield from Zion
your scepter of power;
rule in the midst of all your foes.

A prince from the day of your birth
on the holy mountains;
from the womb before the dawn I begot you.

The LORD has sworn an oath
and will not change.
"You are a priest for ever,
a priest like Melchizedek of old."

The Master standing at your right hand
will shatter rulers in the day of wrath,

Will judge all the nations,
will heap high the bodies;
heads shall be scattered far and wide.

He shall drink from the stream by the wayside,
will stand with head held high.

PSALM PRAYER

Lord Jesus Christ,
faithful witness and firstborn from the dead,
ruler of the nations of the earth,
wash away our sins in your blood
and make us a line of royal priests
to praise and serve your God and Father.
To you be honor and glory for ever and ever.
~*Amen.*

READING   *Luke 24:44–48*

Jesus said to them, "These are my words that
I spoke to you while I was still with you—
that everything written about me in the law of
Moses, the prophets, and the psalms must be
fulfilled." Then he opened their minds to understand the scriptures, and he said to them,
"Thus it is written, that the Messiah is to suffer
and to rise from the dead on the third day,
and that repentance and forgiveness of sins is
to be proclaimed in his name to all nations,
beginning from Jerusalem. You are witnesses
of these things."

SILENCE

RESPONSE

Your cross, O Lord! Alleluia!
~Is the tree of life! Alleluia!

CANTICLE OF MARY   *Luke 1:46–55*

Hail, Mary, full of grace, the Lord is with you!
You bore the Son of God, our risen Lord and
Savior! Alleluia!

My soul **+** proclaims the greatness of the Lord.
My spirit sings to God, my saving God,
Who on this day above all others favored me
And raised me up, a light for all to see.

Through me great deeds will God make
    manifest,
And all the earth will come to call me blest.
Unbounded love and mercy sure will I proclaim
For all who know and praise God's holy name.

God's mighty arm, protector of the just,
Will guard the weak and raise them
    from the dust.
But mighty kings will swiftly fall
    from thrones corrupt.
The strong brought low, the lowly lifted up.

Soon will the poor and hungry of the earth
Be richly blest, be given greater worth.
And Israel, as once foretold to Abraham,
Will live in peace throughout the promised land.

All glory be to God, Creator blest,
To Jesus Christ, God's love made manifest,
And to the Holy Spirit, gentle Comforter,
All glory be, both now and evermore. Amen.

INTERCESSIONS

Save your people, Lord, and bless your
inheritance.
~*Govern and uphold them now and always.*

Day by day we bless you.
~*We praise your name for ever.*

Keep us today, Lord, from all sin.
~*Have mercy on us, Lord, have mercy.*

Lord, show us your love and mercy.
~*For we have put our trust in you.*

In you, Lord, is our hope.
~*Let us never hope in vain.*

LORD'S PRAYER

CLOSING PRAYER

In union with the great Mother of God, Mary
   most holy,
and the whole company of heaven,
we venerate the sacred mysteries
of the passion, death and resurrection
of our Lord, God, and Savior Jesus Christ.
May the perfume of his abiding presence
be the fresh fragrance of life itself for
   all humanity,
now and always and for ever and ever.
~Amen.

Peace be with the whole community, and love
with faith, from God the Father **+** and the
Lord Jesus Christ.
~Amen.

MONDAY MORNING

O Lord, **+** open my lips.
~And my mouth shall declare your praise.

Praise God, the creator of heaven and earth.
~Now and always and for ever and ever.

HYMN

PSALM 3

Jesus offered up prayers and supplications to the one who was able to save him from death.

How many are my foes, O LORD!
How many are rising up against me!
How many are saying about me:
"No help will come from God."

But you, LORD, are a shield about me,
my glory, who lift up my head.
I cry aloud to you, LORD.
You answer from your holy mountain.

I lie down to rest and I sleep.
I wake, for you uphold me.
I will not fear even thousands of people
who are ranged on every side against me.

Arise, LORD; save me, my God,
you who strike all my foes on the mouth,
you who break the teeth of the wicked!
O LORD of salvation, bless your people!

PSALM PRAYER

Lord God,
you are our shield and protector
against those who jeer at us
for trusting in you.
Favor your people, Lord,

as you did your servant Jesus,
whom you saved from death,
for the victory is yours,
now and for ever.
~*Amen.*

READING   *Luke 6:20–26*

Jesus said to his disciples:
Blessed are you who are poor,
for yours is the kingdom of God.
Blessed are you who are hungry now,
for you will be filled.
Blessed are you who weep now,
for you will laugh.
Blessed are you when people hate you,
for surely your reward is great in heaven.

But woe to you who are rich,
for you have received your consolation.
Woe to you who are full now,
for you will be hungry.
Woe to you who are laughing now,
for you will mourn and weep.
Woe to you when all speak well of you,
for that is what their ancestors did
    to the false prophets.

SILENCE

Send forth your light and your truth.
~*Let them bring me to your holy mountain.*

CANTICLE OF THE THREE YOUTHS
Daniel 3:52–57

> *Blest be God's holy and wonderful name.*

Blest are you, God of our ancestors,
praised and glorified above all for ever!
Blest be your holy and wonderful name,
praised and glorified above all for ever!

Blest are you in your temple of glory,
praised and glorified above all for ever!
Blest are you enthroned on the cherubim,
praised and glorified above all for ever!

Blest are you who look into the depths,
praised and glorified above all for ever!
Blest are you above the vault of heaven,
praised and glorified above all for ever!

Bless the Lord, sing to God's glory,
all things fashioned by God's mighty hand.
Bless the Father, the Son, and the Holy Spirit,
praised and glorified above all for ever!

LORD'S PRAYER

CLOSING PRAYER

Lord Jesus,
splendor of the eternal Father,
full of light and glory,
you are the true light that illumines all creation.
Be the light of our hearts and minds,
rescue us from evil passions,
and help us to do what is right and true
in your holy sight.
You live and reign now and for ever.
~*Amen.*

May the God of hope fill us with all joy and
peace in believing so that by the power of the
Holy Spirit **+** we may abound in hope.
~*Amen.*

MONDAY EVENING

God **+** is light and life.
~*There is no darkness in God at all.*

HYMN

PSALM 4

The Lord hears me whenever I call.

When I call, answer me, O God of justice;
from anguish you released me, have mercy and
    hear me!

You rebels, how long will your hearts be closed,
will you love what is futile and seek what
    is false?

It is the LORD who grants favors to those who
    are merciful;
the LORD hears me whenever I call.

Tremble; do not sin: ponder on your bed
    and be still.
Make justice your sacrifice and trust
    in the LORD.

"What can bring us happiness?" many say.
Lift up the light of your face on us, O LORD.

You have put into my heart a greater joy
than they have from abundance of corn and
    new wine.

I will lie down in peace and sleep comes at once
for you alone, LORD, make me dwell in safety.

PSALM PRAYER

Faithful God,
look on the face of your Christ
and listen to our prayers.
May we sleep secure at night,
safe in your everlasting arms.
We ask this through the same Christ our Lord.
~*Amen.*

READING   *2 Corinthians 5:1, 6–8*

Brothers and sisters, we know that if the earthly
tent we live in is destroyed, we have a building
from God, a house not made with hands,
eternal in the heavens. So we are always confi-
dent; even though we know that while we
are at home in the body we are away from the
Lord—for we walk by faith, not by sight.
Yes, we do have confidence, and we would
rather be away from the body and at home with
the Lord.

SILENCE

RESPONSE

Let my prayer arise before you like incense.
~*The raising of my hands like an evening
oblation.*

CANTICLE OF THE FIRSTBORN
Colossians 1:15 – 20

The Word was with God and the Word was God.

Christ is the image of the invisible God,
the firstborn of all creation;
for in him all things in heaven and on earth
   were created,
things visible and invisible,
whether thrones or dominions or rulers
   or powers
—all things have been created through him and
   for him.

He himself is before all things,
and in him all things hold together.
He is the head of the body, the church;
he is the beginning, the firstborn from the dead,
so that he might come to have first place
   in everything.

For in him
all the fullness of God was pleased to dwell,
and through him God was pleased
to reconcile to himself all things,
whether on earth or in heaven,
by making peace through the blood of his cross.

Glory to God: Creator, Redeemer, and Sanctifier,
now and always and for ever and ever. Amen.

INTERCESSIONS

For a night that is perfect, holy, peaceful and
blameless, let us pray to the Lord.
~*Lord, have mercy.*

For an angel of peace to guard our souls
and bodies,
~*Lord, have mercy.*

For the pardon of all our sins and offenses,
~*Lord, have mercy.*

For what is good and profitable to our souls,
~*Lord, have mercy.*

For a painless and peaceful death, and for
trust in God's judgment,
~*Lord, have mercy.*

LORD'S PRAYER

CLOSING PRAYER

Heavenly Father,
even darkness is not dark to you
and night shines bright as day.
Into your hands we commend our lives
    and our labors;
grant us a quiet night, a perfect end,
and peace at the last,
through Jesus Christ our Lord.
~*Amen.*

May the God of hope fill us with all joy and
peace in believing so that by the power of the
Holy Spirit + we may abound in hope.
~*Amen.*

TUESDAY MORNING

O Lord, + open my lips.
~*And my mouth shall declare your praise.*

Blessed be the reign of God: Father, Son, and
Holy Spirit.
~*Now and always and for ever and ever.*

HYMN

PSALM 19

The dawn from on high shall break upon us.

The heavens proclaim the glory of God,
and the firmament shows forth the work of
   God's hands.
Day unto day takes up the story
and night unto night makes known the message.

No speech, no word, no voice is heard
yet their span extends through all the earth,
their words to the utmost bounds of the world.

There God has placed a tent for the sun;
it comes forth like a bridegroom coming from
   his tent,
rejoices like a champion to run its course.

At the end of the sky is the rising of the sun;
to the furthest end of the sky is its course.
There is nothing concealed from its burning heat.

PSALM PRAYER

Lord Jesus Christ,
sun of righteousness,
shine on those who sit in darkness
and the shadow of death,
for you are the morning star of the universe,
the light and life of the world,
and we proclaim your glory,
now and for ever.
~*Amen.*

READING *Luke 6:27–31*

Jesus said to his disciples, "Love your enemies,
do good to those who hate you, bless those
who curse you, pray for those who abuse you.
If anyone strikes you on the cheek, offer the
other also; and from anyone who takes away
your coat do not withhold even your shirt.
Give to everyone who begs from you; and if
anyone takes away your goods, do not ask for

them again. Do to others as you would have them do to you."

SILENCE

RESPONSE
O God, arise above the heavens.
~*May your glory shine on earth!*

CANTICLE OF THE THREE YOUTHS
Daniel 3:56–73

Creation eagerly awaits the full revelation of God in Christ.

Bless the Lord, sing to God's glory,
all things fashioned by God's mighty hand;
Praise God's strength, sing to God's name,
in the present age and in eternity.

Praise the Lord, all you holy angels,
who assist with reverence at God's holy throne.
Let the blue skies bless the Lord,
and all the heavenly sphere embraces.

Bless the Lord, all you waters,
residing above the heavens;
All the great powers of the Lord,
sing his praises for ever.

Let the sun and moon bless the Lord,
they whose rays put to flight the darkness.
Let the great and brilliant stars
give their light to praise God's greatness.

Bless the Lord, all heavenly dew,
bless the Lord, every drop of moisture.
Bless the Lord, all mighty winds,
you ministers of God's majesty.

Bless the Lord all fire and heat,
drying the earth in summer time.
Bless the Lord, all icy blasts,
bringing snow and ice in winter.

Bless the Lord, all mists and frosts,
which crown the peaks of mountains.
Let each day and night of the year
and changing seasons bless the Lord.

Bless the Lord at all times,
in the morning and in the evening.
And may the dark clouds bless the Lord,
through the terror of the lightning.

Let us bless the Father, the Son, and
    the Holy Spirit,
one holy and undivided Trinity;
Blessed are you, Lord, in the highest heavens,
reigning supreme over all creation.

LORD'S PRAYER

CLOSING PRAYER

Creator of heaven and earth,
you fashioned the powers of human reasoning
and of rational speech.
Accept our hymns of praise
that we offer in union with all creation,
for all the powers of heaven and earth
acclaim and exalt you, now and for ever.
~*Amen.*

May the God of peace sanctify us, and
may our spirit, soul and body **+** be kept
sound and blameless at the coming of
our Lord Jesus Christ.
~*Amen.*

TUESDAY EVENING

The Word **+** was the source of life.
~*And this life brought light to all.*

HYMN

PSALM 16

You will not leave my soul among the dead.

Preserve me, God, I take refuge in you.
I say to you LORD: "You are my God.
My happiness lies in you alone."

You have put into my heart a marvelous love
for the faithful ones who dwell in your land.
Those who choose other gods increase
    their sorrows.
Never will I offer their offerings of blood.
Never will I take their name upon my lips.

O LORD, it is you who are my portion and cup,
it is you yourself who are my prize.
The lot marked out for me is my delight,
welcome indeed is the heritage that falls to me!

I will bless you, LORD, you give me counsel,
and even at night direct my heart.
I keep you, LORD, ever in my sight;
since you are at my right hand, I shall stand firm.

And so my heart rejoices, my soul is glad;
even my body shall rest in safety.
For you will not leave my soul among the dead,
nor let your beloved know decay.

You will show me the path of life,
the fullness of joy in your presence,
at your right hand happiness for ever.

PSALM PRAYER

Preserve, O God, those who take refuge in you,
our welcome portion and our inheritance.
Liberate us from the idols of our culture
and assure us of your saving presence,
for you show us the path of life:
the fullness of joy at your side for ever.
~*Amen.*

READING   *2 Corinthians 5:17–18*

Sisters and brothers, if anyone is in Christ,
there is a new creation: everything old has
passed away; see, everything has become new!
All this is from God, who reconciled us through
Christ to God, and has given us the ministry
of reconciliation.

SILENCE

RESPONSE

Have mercy on me, God, have mercy.
~*In the shadow of your wings I take refuge.*

CANTICLE OF THE MYSTERY OF CHRIST
1 Timothy 3:16; 6:15–16

Great is the mystery of our religion!

Christ Jesus our Lord was manifested in
    the flesh:
and was vindicated in the Spirit;
he was seen by angels:
and proclaimed among the nations;
he was believed on in the world:
and was taken up in glory.

He will be revealed in due time by God:
the blessed and only ruler, the sovereign Lord
    of all,
who alone has immortality:
and dwells in unapproachable light,
whom no one has ever seen or can see:
to whom alone be honor and might for ever
    and ever.

INTERCESSIONS

Lord Jesus Christ, God from God, Light from
Light, through whom all things were made:
~*Be our light and our salvation.*

Lord Jesus Christ, source of life and holiness:
~*Be our light and our salvation.*

Lord Jesus Christ, faithful preacher and
guardian of the gospel:
~*Be our light and our salvation.*

Lord Jesus Christ, salt of the earth and light of
the world:
~*Be our light and our salvation.*

Lord Jesus Christ, the beginning and the end,
the first and the last:
~*Be our light and our salvation.*

LORD'S PRAYER

CLOSING PRAYER

Lord our God,
whose power is beyond all words to describe,
whose mercy is without limits,
and whose love for us is beyond all telling:
Look down upon us
and in your kindness grant to all,
the riches of your compassion and mercy;
through Christ our Lord.
~*Amen.*

May the God of peace sanctify us, and
may our spirit, soul and body **+** be kept
sound and blameless at the coming of
our Lord Jesus Christ.
~*Amen.*

O Lord, + open my lips.
~*And my mouth shall declare your praise.*

Glory to God in the highest.
~*And peace to God's people on earth.*

HYMN

PSALM 36:6–12

In your light, O Lord, we see light.

Your love, LORD, reaches to heaven,
your truth to the skies.
Your justice is like God's mountain,
your judgments like the deep.

To mortals and beasts you give protection.
O LORD, how precious is your love.
My God, the children of the earth
find refuge in the shelter of your wings.

They feast on the riches of your house;
they drink from the stream of your delight.
In you is the source of life
and in your light we see light.

Keep on loving those who know you,
doing justice for upright hearts.
Let the foot of the proud not crush me
nor the hand of the wicked cast me out.

Psalm Prayer

Light and life of the world,
shelter us under the wings
of your Son's cross,
as we marvel at your justice and mercy
and rejoice in your protection,
through the same Christ our Lord.
~*Amen.*

READING   *Luke 6:32–35*

Jesus said to his disciples: "If you love those
who love you, what credit is that to you?
For even sinners love those who love them.
If you do good to those who do good to you,
what credit is that to you? For even sinners
do the same. If you lend to those from whom
you hope to receive, what credit is that to
you? Even sinners lend to sinners, to receive as
much again. But love your enemies, do good,
and lend, expecting nothing in return. Your
reward will be great, and you will be children of
the Most High, who is kind to the ungrateful
and the wicked."

SILENCE

RESPONSE
I will sing of your strength.
~*And each morning acclaim your love.*

CANTICLE OF THE THREE YOUTHS
Daniel 3:74–87

Creation shares the glorious freedom of the children of God.

Bless the Lord, sing to God's glory,
all things fashioned by God's mighty hand.
Praise God's strength, sing to God's name,
in the present age and in eternity.

Let the earth and all that is in it
praise the greatness of the Lord.
Let human beings do all within their power
to extol the glory of God's name.

Let the towering mountains bless the Lord,
with the forests and the lowly hills.
Let the flowers and the plants bless the Lord,
every growing thing earth yields.

Bless the Lord, all flowing fountains,
springing from far below the earth.
Bless the Lord, seas and rivers,
whose waters carry our laden ships.

Bless the Lord, you fish and sea monsters,
all creatures living in the waters.
Bless the Lord, all you winged creatures,
who fly the heavens majestically.

Bless the Lord, all you beasts of the earth,
both the wild and the tame.
Bless the Lord, all you human creatures,
and praise his goodness eternally.

Let us bless the Father, the Son, and
    the Holy Spirit,
one holy and undivided Trinity;
Blessed are you, Lord, in the highest heavens,
reigning supreme over all creation.

LORD'S PRAYER

CLOSING PRAYER

Holy and immortal God,
dwelling among the saints,
the seraphim praise you,
the cherubim sing your glory,
and all the powers of heaven and earth
fall down in adoration before you.
Allow us, sinful as we are,
to stand before your holy altar
and to offer you the worship you deserve,
through the merits of Christ our Savior,

who lives and reigns with you and
   the Holy Spirit,
now and for ever.
~*Amen.*

May the Lord **+** direct our hearts in the love of
God and the patience of Christ.
~*Amen.*

WEDNESDAY EVENING

Jesus Christ **+** is the light of the world.
~*A light no darkness can extinguish.*

HYMN

PSALM 23

*I am the good shepherd, I know mine and mine
know me.*

LORD, you are my shepherd;
there is nothing I shall want.
Fresh and green are the pastures
where you give me repose.
Near restful waters you lead me,
to revive my drooping spirit.

You guide me along the right path;
you are true to your name.
If I should walk in the valley of darkness
no evil would I fear.
You are there with your crook and your staff;
with these you give me comfort.

You have prepared a banquet for me
in the sight of my foes.
My head you have anointed with oil;
my cup is overflowing.

Surely goodness and kindness shall follow me
all the days of my life.
In the LORD's own house shall I dwell
for ever and ever.

PSALM PRAYER

Good Shepherd of your people,
refresh us with the waters of the Spirit
and lead us to the sweet repose of eternity.
May our comfort be the staff
that blossomed in the house of David.
Anoint our heads with the oil of chrism
and feed us with the bread and wine
   from your table
that we may dwell in your house
for ever and ever.
~*Amen.*

READING   *Galatians 3:27–28*

Sisters and brothers, as many of you as were
baptized into Christ have clothed yourselves
with Christ. There is no longer Jew or
Greek, there is no longer slave or free, there
is no longer male and female; for all of you
are one in Christ Jesus.

SILENCE

RESPONSE

Let me live in your sanctuary all my life;
~Let me find safety under your wings.

CANTICLE OF THE LAMB
Revelation 4:11; 5:9–10, 12

*Jesus is the Lamb of God who takes away the
sins of the world.*

You are worthy, our Lord and God,
to receive glory and honor and power,
for you created all things,
and by your will they existed and were created.

You are worthy to take the scroll
and to open its seals,
for you were slaughtered
and by your blood you ransomed for God
saints from every tribe and language
and people and nation.

You have made them to be a kingdom and priests
serving our God,
and they will reign on earth.

Worthy is the Lamb
that was slaughtered
to receive power and wealth
and wisdom and might
and honor and glory and blessing!

INTERCESSIONS

Show us your mercy, O Lord.
~And grant us your salvation.

Clothe your ministers with righteousness.
~Let your people sing with joy.

Give peace, O Lord, in all the world.
~For only in you can we live in safety.

Lord, keep this nation under your care.
~And guide us in the way of justice and truth.

Let your way be known upon earth.
~Your saving health among all nations.

Let not the needy, O Lord, be forgotten.
~Nor the hope of the poor be taken away.

Create in us clean hearts, O God.
~And sustain us with your Holy Spirit.

LORD'S PRAYER

CLOSING PRAYER

Keep watch, dear Lord,
with those who work, or watch,
or weep this night,
and give your angels charge
over those who sleep.
Tend the sick, Lord Christ;
give rest to the weary, bless the dying,
soothe the suffering, pity the afflicted,
shield the joyous;
and all for your love's sake.
~*Amen.*

May the Lord + direct our hearts in the love of
God and the patience of Christ.
~*Amen.*

THURSDAY MORNING

O Lord, + open my lips.
~*And my mouth shall declare your praise.*

Bless God, night and day.
~*Give praise and glory.*

HYMN

PSALM 51:3-19

God be merciful to me, a sinner.

Have mercy on me, God, in your kindness.
In your compassion blot out my offense.
O wash me more and more from my guilt
and cleanse me from my sin.

My offenses truly I know them;
my sin is always before me.
Against you, you alone, have I sinned;
what is evil in your sight I have done.

That you may be justified when you give
    sentence
and be without reproach when you judge,
O see, in guilt I was born,
a sinner was I conceived.

Indeed you love truth in the heart;
then in the secret of my heart teach me wisdom.
O purify me, then I shall be clean;
O wash me, I shall be whiter than snow.

Make me hear rejoicing and gladness
that the bones you have crushed may revive.
From my sins turn away your face
and blot out all my guilt.

A pure heart create for me, O God,
put a steadfast spirit within me.
Do not cast me away from your presence,
nor deprive me of your holy spirit.

Give me again the joy of your help;
with a spirit of fervor sustain me,
that I may teach transgressors your ways
and sinners may return to you.

O rescue me, God, my helper,
and my tongue shall ring out your goodness.
O Lord, open my lips
and my mouth shall declare your praise.

For in sacrifice you take no delight,
burnt offering from me you would refuse;
my sacrifice, a contrite spirit,
a humbled, contrite heart you will not spurn.

PSALM PRAYER

Almighty and merciful Father,
when King David repented before you
in sackcloth and ashes,
you poured out on him
the healing medicine of your forgiveness.
Reshape our hearts, O God,
and wash us clean in the precious blood
of your dear Son, our Savior Jesus Christ.
~Amen.

READING   *Luke 6:37–38*

Jesus said to his disciples: "Do not judge,
and you will not be judged; do not condemn,
and you will not be condemned. Forgive,
and you will be forgiven; give, and it will be
given to you. A good measure, pressed down,
shaken together, running over, will be put
into your lap; for the measure you give will be
the measure you get back."

SILENCE

RESPONSE

I will always praise your name.
~And day after day fulfill my vows.

CANTICLE OF THE THREE YOUTHS
Daniel 3:82–88

*Praise the holy name, this name beyond
all names.*

Bless the Lord, sing to God's glory,
all things fashioned by God's mighty hand;
Praise God's strength, sing to God's name,
in the present age and in eternity.

O Israel, bless your God continually,
for ever and ever praise God's greatness.
Bless the Lord, all you his priests;
praise God's goodness eternally.

Bless the Lord, all you saints;
bless God faithfully, all you servants.
Bless the Lord, all you holy souls;
you who are humble, love him.

Let everyone sing to God's glory and praise,
from the present moment until eternity.

Let us bless the Father, the Son, and
    the Holy Spirit,
one holy and undivided Trinity;
Blessed are you, Lord, in the highest heavens,
reigning supreme over all creation.

LORD'S PRAYER

CLOSING PRAYER

Almighty God and Father,
all creation speaks eloquently
of your wonderful works.
Let your glory shine forth in us
that our human life may praise you,
in union with the whole company of heaven,
through Jesus Christ our Lord.
~*Amen.*

May the God of all grace who has called us to
glory in Christ **+** restore, establish and
strengthen us.
~*Amen.*

Jesus Christ ✛ is the light and life of the world.
~And gives light to all peoples.

HYMN

PSALM 27:1–9, 13–14

I will sing, I will praise the Lord!

The LORD is my light and my help;
whom shall I fear?
The LORD is the stronghold of my life;
before whom shall I shrink?

When evildoers draw near
to devour my flesh,
it is they, my enemies and foes,
who stumble and fall.

Though an army encamp against me
my heart will not fear.
Though war break out against me
even then would I trust.

There is one thing I ask of the LORD,
for this I long,
to live in the house of the LORD,
all the days of my life,
to savor the sweetness of the LORD,
to behold his temple.

For God makes me safe in his tent
in the day of evil.
God hides me in the shelter of his tent,
on a rock I am secure.

And now my head shall be raised
above my foes who surround me
and I shall offer within God's tent
a sacrifice of joy.

I will sing and make music for the LORD.

O LORD, hear my voice when I call;
have mercy and answer.
Of you my heart has spoken:
"Seek God's face."

It is your face, O LORD, that I seek;
hide not your face.
Dismiss not your servant in anger;
you have been my help.

I am sure I will see the LORD's goodness
in the land of the living.
In the LORD, hold firm and take heart.
Hope in the LORD!

PSALM PRAYER

Abba, dear Father of Jesus,
our risen Lord,
be our light and our salvation,
keep us safe in your church
and enable us to play and sing to you,
now and for ever.
~*Amen.*

READING   *Galatians 4:4–7*

Brothers and sisters, when the fullness of time
had come, God sent the Son, born of a woman,
born under the law, in order to redeem those
who were under the law, so that we might
receive adoption as children. And because you
are children, God has sent the Spirit of the
Son into our hearts, crying, "Abba! Father!"
So you are no longer a slave but a child, and if
a child then also an heir, through God.

SILENCE

RESPONSE

The lands of sunrise and sunset:
~*You fill with your joy.*

CANTICLE OF OUR ADOPTION
Ephesians 1:3 – 6

> *God has made known to us the mystery of
> his will.*

Blessed are you, God and Father of our Lord
    Jesus Christ:
you have blessed us in Christ
with every spiritual blessing
in the heavenly realms.

Even before the world was made
you chose us to be yours in Christ:
that we should be holy and blameless
in your sight.

In love you destined us for adoption
as your children through Christ Jesus:
such was your pleasure and your purpose,
to the praise of your glorious grace:
which you have freely given us
in your beloved Son.

Glory to the Father, and to the Son,
and to the Holy Spirit:
as it was in the beginning, is now,
and will be for ever. Amen.

INTERCESSIONS

Send forth your light and your truth.
~Let these be our guide.

In you is the source of life.
~In your light we see light.

Make us walk in your truth and teach us.
~For you are God our Savior.

Let your face shine on us.
~And save us in your love.

Clothe your priests in righteousness.
~And make your chosen people joyful.

Lord, give your people strength.
~And bless your people with peace.

LORD'S PRAYER

CLOSING PRAYER

Lighten our darkness, O Lord,
and in your great mercy
defend us from all perils and dangers
of this coming night,
for the sake of your only Son,
our Savior Jesus Christ.
~Amen.

May the God of all grace who has called us to eternal glory in Christ **+** restore, establish and strengthen us.
~*Amen.*

FRIDAY MORNING

O Lord, **+** open my lips.
~*And my mouth shall declare your praise.*

We adore you, O Christ, and we bless you.
~*For by your holy cross you have redeemed the world.*

HYMN

PSALM 13

I rely, O Lord, on your constant love.

How long, O LORD, will you forget me?
How long will you hide your face?
How long must I bear grief in my soul,
this sorrow in my heart day and night?
How long shall my enemy prevail?

Look at me, answer me, LORD my God!
Give light to my eyes lest I fall asleep in death,
lest my enemy say: "I have prevailed";
lest my foes rejoice to see my fall.

As for me, I trust in your merciful love.
Let my heart rejoice in your saving help.
Let me sing to you LORD for your goodness
    to me,
sing psalms to your name, O Lord, Most High.

PSALM PRAYER

Gracious God,
author of peace and lover of concord,
to know you is to live,
to serve you is to reign.
Defend us from all the assaults of our enemies,
that we who trust in your protection
may have no foe to fear;
through Jesus Christ our Lord.
~Amen.

READING   *Matthew 12:39–41*

An evil and adulterous generation asks for a sign,
but no sign will be given to it except the sign
of the prophet Jonah. For just as Jonah was three
days and three nights in the belly of the sea
monster, so for three days and three nights the

Son of Man will be in the heart of the earth.
The people of Nineveh will rise up at the judgment with this generation and condemn it,
because they repented at the proclamation of
Jonah, and see, someone greater than Jonah
is here.

SILENCE

RESPONSE

The sign of the cross will appear in the heavens:
~*When the Lord returns in glory.*

CANTICLE OF THE PROPHET JONAH
Jonah 2:1–4, 6–7

> *From deep in the world of the dead I cried
> for help.*

In my distress, O LORD, I called to you,
and you answered me.
From deep in the world of the dead
I cried for help, and you heard me.

You threw me down into the depths,
to the very bottom of the sea,
where the waters were all around me,
and your mighty waves rolled over me.

I thought I had been banished
   from your presence
and would never see you in your
   holy Temple again.
I went down to the very roots of the mountains,
into the land whose gates lock shut for ever.

But you, O LORD my God,
brought me back from the depths alive.
When I felt my life slipping away,
then, O LORD, I prayed to you,
and in your holy Temple you heard me.

To the King of the ages, immortal, invisible, the
   only wise God,
be honor and glory, through Jesus Christ,
for ever and ever. Amen.

LORD'S PRAYER

CLOSING PRAYER

Abba, merciful Father,
look upon this family of yours
for which our Lord Jesus Christ
did not hesitate to hand himself
over to sinners
and to undergo the torment of the cross.
He now lives and reigns with you

and the Holy Spirit,
one God, for ever and ever.
~*Amen.*

May the glorious passion of our Lord Jesus
Christ **+** bring us to the joys of paradise.
~*Amen.*

FRIDAY EVENING

Jesus Christ **+** is the light of the world.
~*A light no darkness can extinguish.*

HYMN

PSALM 54

Abba! Into your hands I commend my spirit.

O God, save me by your name;
by your power, uphold my cause.
O God, hear my prayer;
listen to the words of my mouth.

For the proud have risen against me,
ruthless foes seek my life.
They have no regard for God.

But I have God for my help.
The Lord upholds my life.
Let the evil recoil upon my foes;
you who are faithful, destroy them.

I will sacrifice to you with a willing heart
and praise your name, O LORD, for it is good;
for you have rescued me from all my distress
and my eyes have seen the downfall of my foes.

PSALM PRAYER

God who saves,
David cried out to you
when he was betrayed to King Saul,
and you delivered him from his foes.
Your Son Jesus cried out on the cross
when people jeered and scoffed at him
and you brought him up out of death.
Be our Savior too when we are in danger
and guard our life from those who attack us.
In Jesus' name.
~*Amen.*

READING *Galatians 6:14, 17*

Sisters and brothers, may I never boast of
anything except the cross of our Lord Jesus
Christ, by which the world has been crucified to me, and I to the world. From now
on, let no one make trouble for me; for I
carry the marks of Jesus branded on my body.

Response
Reign from the noble tree of the cross.
~And establish the reign of God in our hearts.

CANTICLE OF THE EXALTED LORD
Philippians 2:6–11

Christ has died, Christ is risen, Christ will come again!

Though he was in the form of God,
Christ Jesus did not regard equality with God
as something to be exploited,
but emptied himself,
taking the form of a slave,
being born in human likeness.

And being found in human form,
he humbled himself
and became obedient to the point of death—
even death on a cross.

Therefore God also highly exalted him
and gave him the name
that is above every name,

so that at the name of Jesus
every knee should bend,
in heaven and on earth
and under the earth,
and every tongue should confess
that Jesus Christ is Lord,
to the glory of God the Father.

INTERCESSIONS

For the exaltation of the precious
and life-giving cross, let us pray to the Lord.
~Lord, have mercy.

For peace in our time,
~Lord, have mercy.

For refugees and prisoners of war,
~Lord, have mercy.

For the sick and the dying,
~Lord, have mercy.

For light and peace for our beloved dead,
~Lord, have mercy.

LORD'S PRAYER

CLOSING PRAYER

Lord Jesus Christ, Son of the living God,
set your passion, your cross, and your death
between your judgment and our souls,

now and in the hour of our death.
In your goodness,
grant mercy and grace to the living
and forgiveness and rest to the dead,
to the church and to the nations peace
    and concord
and to us sinners life and glory without end.
You live and reign now and for ever.
~*Amen.*

May the glorious passion of our Lord Jesus
Christ + bring us to the joys of paradise.
~*Amen.*

SATURDAY MORNING

O Lord + open my lips.
~*And my mouth shall declare your praise.*

Blest be the Lord our God, ruler of the universe.
~*Now and always and for ever and ever.*

HYMN

PSALM 63:1-9

O God, I long for you from break of day.

O God, you are my God, for you I long;
for you my soul is thirsting.
My body pines for you
like a dry, weary land without water.
So I gaze on you in the sanctuary
to see your strength and your glory.

For your love is better than life,
my lips will speak your praise.
So I will bless you all my life,
in your name I will lift up my hands.
My soul shall be filled as with a banquet,
my mouth shall praise you with joy.

On my bed I remember you.
On you I muse through the night
for you have been my help;
in the shadow of your wings I rejoice.
My soul clings to you;
your right hand holds me fast.

PSALM PRAYER

Author of undying light,
quench our thirst for you
from the deep wells of the Spirit,

that our lips may praise you,
our lives reflect you,
and our meditations glorify you
as we rejoice beneath your wings.
We ask this through Christ our Lord.
~*Amen.*

READING *Luke 6:41–42*

Jesus said to his disciples: "Why do you see
the speck in your neighbor's eye, but do
not notice the log in your own eye? Or how
can you say to your neighbor, 'Friend, let me
take out the speck in your eye,' when you
yourself do not see the log in your own eye?
You hypocrite, first take the log out of your
own eye, and then you will see clearly to
take the speck out of your neighbor's eye."

SILENCE

RESPONSE

The ends of the earth stand in awe:
~*At the sight of your wonders.*

CANTICLE OF MOSES AND MIRIAM
Exodus 15:1, 2, 11, 13, 17

Who is like you, O Lord, majestic in holiness?

I will sing to the Lord,
for the Lord has triumphed gloriously:
the horse and its rider
have been thrown into the sea.

The Lord is my strength and my song:
and has become my salvation.
This is my God, whom I will praise:
the God of my forebears whom I will exalt.

Who is like you, O Lord, among the gods:
who is like you majestic in holiness?
Who is like you, O Lord, among the gods:
terrible in glorious deeds and doing wonders?

In your unfailing love you will lead
the people you have redeemed:
in your strength you will
guide them to your holy dwelling.

You will bring them in and plant them
on the mountain of your inheritance:
the place, O Lord,
that you have made for your dwelling,
the sanctuary, O Lord,
that your hands have established:
you, Lord, will reign for ever and ever.

To the King of the ages, immortal, invisible,
the only wise God,
be honor and glory, through Jesus Christ,
for ever and ever. Amen.

LORD'S PRAYER

CLOSING PRAYER

Lord of hosts,
by Moses and Miriam
you led your chosen people
out of the slavery of Egypt
and into the promised land
flowing with milk and honey.
Under the guidance of Jesus and Mary,
conduct your church in safety
through the trials of the world,
the flesh and the devil,
and bring us in joy to the paradise
where you live and reign,
Father, Son, and Holy Spirit,
now and for ever.
~*Amen.*

May the Word made flesh, full of grace and
truth, **+** bless us and keep us.
~*Amen.*

Let us stand to sing the psalms in such a way that our minds are in harmony with our voices.

~Saint Benedict, ca. 480–547

SECOND WEEK

Light and peace ✚ in Jesus Christ our Lord.
~*Thanks be to God.*

HYMN

PSALM 84:1–6, 9–13

*Turn your eyes, O Lord, and look on the face of
your Anointed.*

How lovely is your dwelling place,
LORD, God of hosts.

My soul is longing and yearning,
is yearning for the courts of the LORD.
My heart and my soul ring out their joy
to God, the living God.

The sparrow herself finds a home
and the swallow a nest for her brood;
she lays her young by your altars,
LORD of hosts, my king and my God.

They are happy, who dwell in your house,
for ever singing your praise.
They are happy, whose strength is in you,
in whose hearts are the roads to Zion.

O LORD God of hosts, hear my prayer,
give ear, O God of Jacob.
Turn your eyes, O God, our shield,
look on the face of your anointed.

One day within your courts
is better than a thousand elsewhere.
The threshold of the house of God
I prefer to the dwellings of the wicked.

For the LORD God is a rampart, a shield.
The LORD will give us favor and glory.
The LORD will not refuse any good
to those who walk without blame.

LORD, God of hosts,
happy are those who trust in you!

PSALM PRAYER

Praise, thanksgiving, glory and honor
to the Father who created us,
to the Son who redeemed us,
to the Holy Spirit who sanctifies us.
Blessed be the holy and undivided Trinity,
now and for ever.
~Amen.

READING   *Galatians 5:13–15*

You were called to freedom, brothers and sisters;
only do not use your freedom as an opportunity for self-indulgence, but through love
become slaves to one another. For the whole law
is summed up in a single commandment, "You
shall love your neighbor as yourself." If, however, you bite and devour one another, take care
that you are not consumed by one another.

SILENCE

RESPONSE

Yours is the day and yours is the night.
~*It was you who appointed the light and the sun.*

CANTICLE OF CHRIST OUR PASSOVER
*1 Corinthians 5:7–8; Romans 6:9–11;
1 Corinthians 15:20–22*

*Christ must reign until God defeats all enemies
and puts them under his feet.*

Christ our Passover has been sacrificed for us;
therefore let us keep the feast.
Not with the old leaven, the leaven of malice
and evil,
but with the unleavened bread of sincerity and
truth. Alleluia!

Christ being raised from the dead will
   never die again;
death no longer has dominion over him.
The death that he died, he died to sin,
   once for all;
but the life he lives, he lives to God.
So also consider yourselves dead to sin,
but alive to God in Jesus Christ our Lord.
   Alleluia!

Christ has been raised from the dead,
the first fruits of those who have fallen asleep.
For since by a man came death,
by a man has come also the resurrection
   of the dead.
For as in Adam all die,
so also in Christ shall all be made alive. Alleluia!

Glory to the Father, and to the Son,
and to the Holy Spirit:
as it was in the beginning, is now,
and will be for ever. Amen.

APOSTLES' CREED

INTERCESSIONS

Lord Jesus Christ, king of glory, our light and
our joy:
~*O Savior, save us.*

By the divine power of your precious and life-giving cross:
~*O Savior, save us.*

By your glorious resurrection and wonderful ascension:
~*O Savior, save us.*

By the coming of the Holy Spirit, our advocate and counselor:
~*O Savior, save us.*

By the sacred mysteries of our baptism and the holy eucharist:
~*O Savior, save us.*

LORD'S PRAYER

Let us pray as Jesus taught us:
~*Our Father . . .*

CLOSING PRAYER

Lord Jesus Christ,
you loved us and offered yourself up for us
as an agreeable and fragrant sacrifice to God.
Deliver us from our former way of life
and teach us to conduct ourselves
    as children of light
in all goodness, justice and truth.
You live and reign now and for ever.
~*Amen.*

May the Word made flesh, full of grace and
truth, + bless us and keep us.
~*Amen.*

SUNDAY MORNING

O Lord, + open my lips.
~*And my mouth shall declare your praise.*

Come, let us worship Christ, our risen Lord!
Alleluia!
~*And bow down in adoration! Alleluia!*

HYMN

PSALM 118:1, 5–9, 13–17, 22–24, 29

Alleluia, alleluia, alleluia!

Give thanks to the LORD who is good,
for God's love endures for ever.

I called to the LORD in my distress;
God answered and freed me.
The LORD is at my side; I do not fear.
What can mortals do against me?
The LORD is at my side as my helper;
I shall look down on my foes.

It is better to take refuge in the LORD
than to trust in mortals;
it is better to take refuge in the LORD
than to trust in rulers.

I was thrust down, thrust down and falling,
but the LORD was my helper.
The LORD is my strength and my song;
and has been my savior.
There are shouts of joy and victory
in the tents of the just.

The LORD's right hand has triumphed;
God's right hand has raised me.
The LORD's right hand has triumphed;
I shall not die, I shall live
and recount God's deeds.

The stone which the builders rejected
has become the corner stone.
This is the work of the LORD,
a marvel in our eyes.
This day was made by the LORD;
we rejoice and are glad.

Give thanks to the LORD who is good;
for God's love endures for ever.

PSALM PRAYER
Holy, mighty, and ever-living God,
you sealed a covenant of reconciliation with us

in the mystery of Christ's passing
  from death to life.
May we come to everlasting joy
by the keeping of this day of victory,
through the same Christ our Lord.
~*Amen.*

READING *Matthew 28:16–20*

The eleven disciples went to Galilee, to the
mountain to which Jesus had directed them.
When they saw him, they worshiped him;
but some doubted. And Jesus came and said to
them, "All authority in heaven and on earth
has been given to me. Go therefore and make
disciples of all nations, baptizing them in
the name of the Father and of the Son and of
the Holy Spirit, and teaching them to obey
everything that I have commanded you. And
remember, I am with you always, to the end
of the age."

SILENCE

RESPONSE

By your glorious resurrection, O Lord:
~*Save us from sin and the grave.*

CANTICLE OF ZACHARY *Luke 1:68–79*

Holy, holy, holy! The Lord almighty is holy!
God's glory fills the whole world.

Blest be **+** the Lord, the God of Israel,
Who brings the dawn and darkest night dispels,
Who raises up a mighty savior from the earth,
Of David's line, a son of royal birth.

The prophets tell a story just begun
Of vanquished foe and glorious victory won,
Of promise made to all who keep the law
   as guide:
God's faithful love and mercy will abide.

This is the oath once sworn to Abraham:
All shall be free to dwell upon the land,
Free now to praise, unharmed by the
   oppressor's rod,
Holy and righteous in the sight of God.

And you, my child, this day you shall be called
The promised one, the prophet of our God,
For you will go before the Lord to clear
   the way,
And shepherd all into the light of day.

The tender love God promised from our birth
Is soon to dawn upon this shadowed earth,
To shine on those whose sorrows seem
    to never cease,
To guide our feet into the path of peace.

APOSTLES' CREED

LORD'S PRAYER

Let us pray as Jesus taught us:
~*Our Father* . . .

CLOSING PRAYER

Risen Lord and Christ,
the one mediator between God and humanity,
teach us to lift up our hands and our hearts
reverently in prayer
and to hold to the pattern of sound teaching
delivered to the holy apostles.
To you be the glory for ever.
~*Amen.*

Peace be with the whole community, and love
with faith, from God the Father **+** and the
Lord Jesus Christ.
~*Amen.*

Jesus Christ + is the light of the world.
~*A light no darkness can extinguish.*

HYMN

PSALM 2

Jesus is the conquering lion of the tribe of Judah!
Alleluia!

Why this tumult among nations,
among peoples this useless murmuring?
They arise, the kings of the earth,
princes plot against the LORD and his Anointed.
"Come, let us break their fetters,
come, let us cast off their yoke."

God who sits in the heavens laughs,
the Lord is laughing them to scorn.
Then God will speak in anger,
and in rage will strike them with terror.
"It is I who have set up my king
on Zion, my holy mountain."

The Lord said to me: "You are my Son.
It is I who have begotten you this day.
Ask and I shall bequeath you the nations,
put the ends of the earth in your possession.
With a rod of iron you will break them,
shatter them like a potter's jar."

Now, O kings, understand,
take warning, rulers of the earth;
serve the LORD with awe
and trembling, pay your homage
lest God be angry and you perish;
for suddenly God's anger will blaze.

Blessed are they who put their trust in God.

PSALM PRAYER

Abba, dear Father of Jesus,
your anointed and victorious Son
empowered us by his coming among us
to take our stand for justice.
May the light of faith
shine in our words and actions
as we stand in awe before him,
who lives and reigns with you and
    the Holy Spirit,
now and for ever.
~*Amen.*

READING   *Acts 2:29-30, 32-33*

My friends, nobody can deny that the patriarch David died and was buried; we have his tomb here to this very day. It is clear therefore that he spoke as a prophet who knew that God had sworn to him that one of his own direct descendants should sit on his throne. Now Jesus has been raised by God, and of this we are all witnesses. Exalted at God's right hand he received from the Father the promised Holy Spirit, and all that you now see and hear flows from him.

SILENCE

RESPONSE

The ends of the earth have seen! Alleluia!
~*The victory of our God! Alleluia!*

CANTICLE OF MARY   *Luke 1:46-55*

We turn to you for protection, holy Mother of God. Listen to our prayers and help us in all our needs. Save us from every danger, glorious and blessed Virgin.

My soul + proclaims the greatness of the Lord.
My spirit sings to God, my saving God,
Who on this day above all others favored me
And raised me up, a light for all to see.

Through me great deeds will God make
    manifest,
And all the earth will come to call me blest.
Unbounded love and mercy sure will I proclaim
For all who know and praise God's holy name.

God's mighty arm, protector of the just,
Will guard the weak and raise them
    from the dust.
But mighty kings will swiftly fall
    from thrones corrupt.
The strong brought low, the lowly lifted up.

Soon will the poor and hungry of the earth
Be richly blest, be given greater worth.
And Israel, as once foretold to Abraham,
Will live in peace throughout the promised land.

All glory be to God, Creator blest,
To Jesus Christ, God's love made manifest,
And to the Holy Spirit, gentle Comforter,
All glory be, both now and evermore. Amen.

INTERCESSIONS

Lord Jesus Christ, you died for our sins
and rose for our justification.
~Hear us, risen Lord.

Lord Jesus Christ, you overcame death's sting
and gave fresh life to our fallen world.
~Hear us, risen Lord.

Lord Jesus Christ, you established the new and
eternal covenant in your precious blood.
~Hear us, risen Lord.

Lord Jesus Christ, you set us free from the law
of sin and death.
~Hear us, risen Lord.

Lord Jesus Christ, you are the same yesterday,
today, and for ever.
~Hear us, risen Lord.

LORD'S PRAYER

CLOSING PRAYER

God of the universe,
creator of light and darkness,
origin and preserver of all that exists:
Remember your church,
protect it from all evil,
and perfect it in your love.
Gather it from the four winds
and bring it into your kingdom,
for the sake of Jesus, our risen Lord,
who lives and reigns with you
and the Holy Spirit,
one God, now and for ever.
~Amen.

Peace be with the whole community, and love with faith, from God the Father **+** and the Lord Jesus Christ.
~Amen.

MONDAY MORNING

O Lord, **+** open my lips.
~And my mouth shall declare your praise.

Blest be the God of our ancestors.
~Blest be God's holy name!

HYMN

PSALM 42:2–5, 9

The river of the water of life, bright as crystal.

Like the deer that yearns
for running streams,
so my soul is yearning
for you, my God.

My soul is thirsting for God,
the God of my life;
when can I enter and see
the face of God?

My tears have become my bread,
by night, by day,
as I hear it said all day long:
"Where is your God?"

These things will I remember
as I pour out my soul:
how I would lead the rejoicing crowd
into the house of God,
amid cries of gladness and thanksgiving,
the throng wild with joy.

By day the LORD will send forth
loving kindness;
by night I will sing to the Lord,
praise the God of my life.

PSALM PRAYER

Lord Jesus, my Savior and my God,
give me the water of life to drink,
the free gift of the Spirit
flowing from your Sacred Heart,
for you are good and you love us all,
and we glorify you and your dear Father
and your life-giving Spirit,
now and for ever.
~Amen.

READING *Ephesians 2:4–6*

Brothers and sisters, God, who is rich in mercy, out of the great love with which God loved us even when we were dead through our trespasses, made us alive together with Christ—by grace you have been saved. With Christ God raised us up and enthroned us in the heavenly places in Christ Jesus.

SILENCE

RESPONSE

O God, you are my God,
~For you I long, from early morning.

THE CANTICLE OF HANNAH
1 Samuel 2:1–4, 7–8

God pulls tyrants from their thrones and lifts up the lowly.

My heart exults in the Lord;
my strength is exalted in my God.

There is none holy like the LORD:
there is none beside you, no rock like our God.

For you, O Lord, are a God of knowledge:
and by you our actions are weighed.
The bows of the mighty are broken:
but the feeble gird on strength.

You, Lord, make poor and make rich:
you bring low and you also exalt.

You raise up the poor from the dust:
and lift the needy from the ash-heap.
You make them sit with princes:
and inherit a seat of honor.

For yours, O Lord, are the pillars of the earth:
and on them you have set the world.

Glory to you, Source of all being,
Eternal Word, and Holy Spirit:
as it was in the beginning, is now,
and will be for ever. Amen.

LORD'S PRAYER

CLOSING PRAYER

In your wisdom, O Lord of life and death,
you made mothers of both Hannah and the
    Virgin Mary
to show how you love the poor and humble,
how you sit them with the high and mighty.
Walk with your faithful, Lord,
and reverse all human expectations
to show that you own the universe
and take command of it,
in and through Christ Jesus our Lord.
~*Amen.*

May the God of hope fill us with all joy and
peace in believing so that by the power of the
Holy Spirit + we may abound in hope.
~*Amen.*

MONDAY EVENING

God + is our light and our life.
~*And this light brought life to all.*

HYMN

PSALM 43

I will come to your altar, O God, the God
of my joy.

Defend me, O God, and plead my cause
against a godless nation.
From a deceitful and cunning people
rescue me, O God.

Since you, O God, are my stronghold,
why have you rejected me?
Why do I go mourning
oppressed by the foe?

O send forth your light and your truth;
let these be my guide.
Let them bring me to your holy mountain,
to the place where you dwell.

And I will come to your altar, O God,
the God of my joy.
My redeemer, I will thank you on the harp,
O God, my God.

Why are you cast down, my soul,
why groan within me?
Hope in God; I will praise yet again,
my savior and my God.

PSALM PRAYER

Saving God,
when we feel surrounded
and defeated by life's misfortunes,
send us your light and your truth
and escort us to your holy altar,
the shrine of your undying presence.
In Jesus' name.
~Amen.

READING   *Ephesians 5:18b–20*

Sisters and brothers, be filled with the Spirit, as
you sing psalms and hymns and spiritual songs
among yourselves, singing and making melody

to the Lord in your hearts, giving thanks to
God the Father at all times and for everything
in the name of our Lord Jesus Christ.

SILENCE

RESPONSE

Lift up your hands to the holy place.
~And bless the Lord through the night.

CANTICLE OF CHRIST'S REIGN
Revelation 11:17–18; 12:10–11

Christ will reign for ever and ever!

We give you thanks, Lord God Almighty,
who are and who were,
for you have taken your great power
and begun to reign.

The nations raged,
but your wrath has come,
and the time for judging the dead,
for rewarding your servants,
the prophets and saints,
and all who fear your name,
both small and great,
and for destroying those
who destroy the earth.

Now have come the salvation and the power
and the kingdom of our God
and the authority of his Messiah,
for the accuser of our comrades
has been thrown down,
who accuses them day and night
before our God.

But they have conquered him
by the blood of the Lamb
and by the word of their testimony,
for they did not cling to life
even in the face of death.

To the King of ages, immortal, invisible,
the only wise God,
be honor and glory, through Jesus Christ,
for ever and ever. Amen.

INTERCESSIONS

For the peace and stability of the whole world,
let us pray to the Lord.
~*Lord, hear our prayer.*

For our country and every country
and for peace among nations,
~*Lord, hear our prayer.*

For the reunion of all the churches of Christ,
~*Lord, hear our prayer.*

For the union of charity, the bond of perfection,
the gift of the Spirit,
~*Lord, hear our prayer.*

For a sinless life by day and by night,
~*Lord, hear our prayer.*

LORD'S PRAYER

CLOSING PRAYER

Visit our hearts and our homes,
O God of peace,
and free us from the snares
of the prince of darkness.
Commit us to the watchful care
of your holy angels,
and send your blessing upon us,
through Jesus Christ our Lord.
~*Amen.*

May the God of hope fill us with all joy and
peace in believing so that by the power of the
Holy Spirit **+** we may abound in hope.
~*Amen.*

O Lord, **+** open my lips.
~*And my mouth shall declare your praise.*

Glory to the Father, glory to the Son.
~*Glory to the Holy Spirit.*

HYMN

PSALM 8

God has put all things under Christ's feet.

How great is your name, O LORD our God,
through all the earth!

Your majesty is praised above the heavens;
on the lips of children and of babes
you have found praise to foil your enemy,
to silence the foe and the rebel.

When I see the heavens, the work of your hands,
the moon and the stars which you arranged,
what are we that you should keep us in mind,
mere mortals that you care for us?

Yet you have made us little less than gods;
and crowned us with glory and honor,
you gave us power over the work of your hands,
put all things under our feet.

All of them, sheep and cattle,
yes, even the savage beasts,
birds of the air, and fish
that make their way through the waters.

How great is your name, O LORD our God,
through all the earth!

PSALM PRAYER

Lord our God,
you created the world for us
and gave us charge over all your creatures.
Teach us to respect and preserve your gifts
and to thank you with all our hearts
for the dignity of our humanity.
We ask this through Christ our Lord,
to whom you have subjected all things,
now and for ever.
~*Amen.*

READING   *Ephesians 6:11, 14–17*

Sisters and brothers, put on the whole armor of
God, so that you may be able to stand against
the wiles of the devil. Stand and fasten the belt
of truth around your waist, and put on the
breastplate of righteousness. As shoes for your
feet put on whatever will make you ready to
proclaim the gospel of peace. With all of these,
take the shield of faith, with which you will

be able to quench all the flaming arrows of the evil one. Take the helmet of salvation, and the sword of the Spirit, which is the word of God.

SILENCE

RESPONSE

In the morning I offer you my prayer.
~*In the morning you hear me.*

CANTICLE OF KING DAVID
1 Chronicles 29:10a–13

Praise God, the creator of all things!

Blessed are you, O LORD,
the God of our ancestor Israel,
forever and ever.
Yours, O LORD, are the greatness, the power,
the glory, the victory, and the majesty;

For all that is in the heavens and on the earth
is yours;
yours is the kingdom, O LORD,
and you are exalted as head above all.

Riches and honor come from you,
and you rule over all.
In your hand are power and might;
and it is in your hand to make great
and to give strength to all.

And now, our God, we give thanks to you
and praise your glorious name.

Glory to God: Creator, Redeemer, and Sanctifier,
now and always and for ever and ever. Amen.

LORD'S PRAYER

CLOSING PRAYER

Holy and majestic Father,
the praise of all your saints and angels,
be mindful of those who offer you
their morning worship.
Help and protect them
throughout the coming day,
and make them genuine disciples
of your dear Son, our Savior,
who lives and reigns with you and
   the Holy Spirit,
now and for ever.
~*Amen.*

May the God of peace sanctify us wholly, and
may our spirit, soul and body **+** be kept sound
and blameless at the coming of our Lord Jesus
Christ.
~*Amen.*

The Word **+** was the source of life.
~And this life brought life to all.

HYMN

PSALM 29

Glory to God and peace to God's people!

O give the LORD, you children of God,
give the LORD glory and power;
give the LORD the glory of his name.
Adore the LORD resplendent and holy.

The LORD's voice resounding on the waters,
the LORD on the immensity of waters;
the voice of the LORD full of power,
the voice of the LORD, full of splendor.

The LORD's voice shattering the cedars,
the LORD shatters the cedars of Lebanon,
makes Lebanon leap like a calf
and Sirion like a young wild ox.

The LORD's voice flashes flames of fire.
The LORD's voice shaking the wilderness,
the LORD shakes the wilderness of Kadesh;
the LORD's voice rending the oak tree
and stripping the forest bare.

The God of glory thunders.
In his temple they all cry: "Glory!"
The LORD sat enthroned over the flood;
the LORD sits as king for ever.

The LORD will give strength to his people,
the LORD will bless his people with peace.

PSALM PRAYER

God of glory and majesty,
pour out your Spirit upon us
like a rushing wind and a flaming fire.
Give us strength to do your will
and the peace that passes all understanding.
We ask this through Christ our Lord.
~Amen.

READING   *Titus 2:11–13*

For the grace of God has appeared, bringing
salvation to all, training us to renounce impiety
and worldly passions, and in the present age
to live lives that are self-controlled, upright, and
godly, while we wait for the blessed hope and
the manifestation of the glory of our great God
and Savior, Jesus Christ.

SILENCE

RESPONSE

I will bless you, LORD, you give me counsel.
~*And even at night direct my heart.*

CANTICLE OF THE REDEEMED
Revelation 15:3-4

Great and wonderful are your deeds!

Great and amazing are your deeds,
Lord God the Almighty!
Just and true are your ways,
King of the nations!

Lord, who will not fear
and glorify your name?
For you alone are holy.

All nations will come
and worship before you,
for your judgments have been revealed.

Glory to the Father, and to the Son,
and to the Holy Spirit:
as it was in the beginning, is now,
and will be for ever. Amen.

INTERCESSIONS

For faithful witnesses to the Good News of the
gospel, let us pray to the Lord.
~*Lord, hear our prayer.*

For devoted bishops, priests and deacons,
~*Lord, hear our prayer.*

For all the ministries of teaching and healing,
~*Lord, hear our prayer.*

For just and enlightened governments,
~*Lord, hear our prayer.*

For the hungry and imprisoned, the persecuted
and afflicted,
~*Lord, hear our prayer.*

For the sick and the dying and the
faithful departed,
~*Lord, hear our prayer.*

LORD'S PRAYER

CLOSING PRAYER

Lord of all days and seasons,
hear our evening prayer,
that freed from the dangers of sin
we may always walk in your light,
through Jesus Christ our Lord.
~*Amen.*

May the God of peace sanctify us, and
may our spirit, soul and body **+** be kept
sound and blameless at the coming of
our Lord Jesus Christ.
~*Amen.*

O Lord, **+** open my lips.
~And my mouth shall declare your praise.

Blest be the name of the Lord.
~Now and for ever.

HYMN

PSALM 65:2-9

*You keep your pledge with wonders, O God
our Savior.*

To you our praise is due
in Zion, O God.
To you we pay our vows,
you who hear our prayer.

To you all flesh will come
with its burden of sin.
Too heavy for us, our offences,
but you wipe them away.

Blessed those whom you choose and call
to dwell in your courts.
We are filled with the blessings of your house,
of your holy temple.

You keep your pledge with wonders,
O God our savior,
the hope of all the earth
and of far distant isles.

You uphold the mountains with your strength,
you are girded with power.
You still the roaring of the seas,
the roaring of their waves,
and the tumult of the peoples.

The ends of the earth stand in awe
at the sight of your wonders.
The lands of sunrise and sunset
you fill with your joy.

PSALM PRAYER

At every moment, O God,
you are listening to our prayers
and forgiving our sins.
Help us to take joy
in your presence and power
and fill us with the holiness
that comes from you alone.
In Jesus' name.
~*Amen.*

READING   *Colossians 3:12–13*

Brothers and sisters, as God's chosen ones, holy
and beloved, clothe yourselves with compassion, kindness, humility, meekness, and patience.
Bear with one another and, if anyone has a
complaint against another, forgive each other;
just as the Lord has forgiven you, so you also
must forgive.

SILENCE

RESPONSE

When I awake I shall see your face.
~And be filled with the sight of your glory.

CANTICLE OF JUDITH   *Judith 16:13–15*

O Lord, my God, how great you are!

I will sing to my God a new song:
O Lord, you are great and glorious,
wonderful in strength, invincible.

Let all your creatures serve you,
for you spoke, and they were made.
You sent forth your spirit, and it formed them;
there is none that can resist your voice.

For the mountains shall be shaken to their
    foundations with the waters;
before your glance the rocks shall melt like wax.
But to those who fear you
you show mercy.

To the King of the ages, immortal, invisible,
the only wise God,
be honor and glory, through Jesus Christ,
for ever and ever. Amen.

LORD'S PRAYER

CLOSING PRAYER

Living and loving God,
in your goodness you give us a new day
to love and serve you.
Keep us from all sin and danger,
make us aware of our neighbor,
and fill us with your inspiration,
through Jesus, our blessed Savior.
~*Amen.*

May the Lord + direct our hearts in the love of
God and the patience of Christ.
~*Amen.*

Light and peace **+** in Jesus Christ our Lord.
~Thanks be to God.

HYMN

PSALM 77:2–16, 21

You are the God who works wonders among
the nations.

I cry aloud to God,
cry aloud to God to hear me.
In the day of my distress I sought the Lord.
My hands were raised at night without ceasing;
my soul refused to be consoled.
I remembered my God and I groaned.
I pondered and my spirit fainted.

You withheld sleep from my eyes.
I was troubled, I could not speak.
I thought of the days of long ago
and remembered the years long past.
At night I mused within my heart.
I pondered and my spirit questioned.

"Will the Lord reject us for ever
and no longer show favor to us?
Has God's love vanished for ever?
Has God's promise come to an end?
Does God forget to be gracious,
or in anger withhold compassion?"

I said: "This is what causes my grief,
that the way of the Most High has changed."
I remember the deeds of the LORD,
I remember your wonders of old,
I muse on all your works
and ponder your mighty deeds.

Your ways, O God, are holy.
What god is great as our God?
You are the God who works wonders.
You showed your power among the peoples.
Your strong arm redeemed your people,
the children of Jacob and Joseph.

You guided your people like a flock
by the hand of Moses and Aaron.

PSALM PRAYER

In our distress, O God,
we forget your divine providence
and begin to brood and question.
Help us to recall your mighty acts
and to rejoice again in your love for us.
We ask this through Christ our Lord.
~*Amen.*

READING *1 Thessalonians 4:13–14*

We do not want you to be uninformed, brothers
and sisters, about those who have died, so
that you may not grieve as others do who have
no hope. For since we believe that Jesus died
and rose again, even so, through Jesus, God will
bring with him those who have died.

SILENCE

RESPONSE

You, O LORD, are my lamp.
~*My God who lightens my darkness.*

CANTICLE OF CONSOLATION
2 Corinthians 1:3–7

It is God who establishes us in Christ and has anointed us.

Blessed be the God and the Father of our
    Lord Jesus Christ,
the Father of mercies and the God of
    all consolation,
who consoles us in all our affliction,
so that we may be able to console
those who are in any affliction with
    the consolation
with which we ourselves are consoled by God.

For just as the sufferings of Christ are
    abundant for us,
so also our consolation is abundant
    through Christ.
If we are being afflicted,
it is for your consolation and salvation;
if we are being consoled,
it is for your consolation,
which you experience when you patiently
    endure
the same sufferings that we are also suffering.

Glory to the holy and undivided Trinity:
now and always and for ever and ever. Amen.

INTERCESSIONS

For the church universal and its continuing renewal, let us pray to the Lord.
~*Lord, have mercy.*

For humanity's creative vision and inventive skill,
~*Lord, have mercy.*

For the sick and handicapped and for the ministries of care and healing,
~*Lord, have mercy.*

For all that sets us free from pain, fear and distress,
~*Lord, have mercy.*

For the assurance that God's mercy knows no limit,
~*Lord, have mercy.*

LORD'S PRAYER

CLOSING PRAYER

Immortal, holy and living God,
fill your church with life,
the church that puts its trust
in the power of your name.
Rescue us from our distress
and teach us to acknowledge you

with a willing heart,
through Jesus Christ our Lord.
~*Amen.*

May the Lord **+** direct our hearts in the love of
God and the patience of Christ.
~*Amen.*

THURSDAY MORNING

O Lord, **+** open my lips.
~*And my mouth shall declare your praise.*

Blest be the holy and undivided Trinity.
~*Now and always and for ever and ever.*

HYMN

PSALM 67

May all nations learn your saving help.

O God, be gracious and bless us
and let your face shed its light upon us.
So will your ways be known upon earth
and all nations learn your saving help.

Let the peoples praise you, O God;
let all the peoples praise you.

Let the nations be glad and exult
for you rule the world with justice.
With fairness you rule the peoples,
you guide the nations on earth.

Let the peoples praise you, O God;
let all the peoples praise you.

The earth has yielded its fruit
for God, our God, has blessed us.
May God still give us blessing
till the ends of the earth stand in awe.

Let the peoples praise you, O God;
let all the peoples praise you.

Psalm Prayer

Christ our Lord,
let your glorious face shine on us
and be a beacon of hope to the whole world.
You are our Savior here and now,
and our joy for ever and ever.
~Amen.

READING *Philippians 4:4–7*

Sisters and brothers, rejoice in the Lord
always; again I will say, Rejoice. Let your
gentleness be known to everyone. The Lord
is near. Do not worry about anything, but
in everything by prayer and supplication with

thanksgiving let your requests be made known to God. And the peace of God, which surpasses all understanding, will guard your hearts and minds in Christ Jesus.

SILENCE

RESPONSE

The LORD is my light and my salvation.
~*Whom shall I fear?*

CANTICLE OF WISDOM *Proverbs 9:1–6, 10*

Those who find me find life, and anyone who hates me finds death.

Wisdom has built her house,
she has hewn her seven pillars.
She has slaughtered her animals,
she has mixed her wine,
she has also set her table.

She has sent out her servant-girls,
she calls from the highest places in the town,
"You that are simple, turn in here!"

To those without sense she says,
"Come, eat of my bread
and drink of the wine I have mixed.
Lay aside immaturity, and live,
and walk in the way of insight."

The fear of the LORD is the beginning
   of wisdom,
and the knowledge of the Holy One is insight.

Glory to you, Source of all being,
Eternal Word, and Holy Spirit:
as it was in the beginning, is now,
and will be for ever. Amen.

LORD'S PRAYER

CLOSING PRAYER

Heavenly Father,
by whose wisdom we are created
and by whose providence we are governed,
give us the grace to offer you thanks
to the best of our ability,
for unless you direct us by your Holy Spirit,
we do not know how to address you
as we ought.
We ask this through Christ our Lord.
~*Amen.*

May the God of all grace who has called us to
eternal glory in Christ + restore, establish and
strengthen us.
~*Amen.*

I am + the light of the world.
~*Whoever follows me will have the light of life.*

HYMN

PSALM 91

God's wings will conceal you.

Those who dwell in the shelter of the Most High
and abide in the shade of the Almighty
say to the LORD: "My refuge,
my stronghold, my God in whom I trust!"

It is God who will free you from the snare
of the fowler who seeks to destroy you;
God will conceal you with his pinions,
and under his wings you will find refuge.

You will not fear the terror of the night
nor the arrow that flies by day,
nor the plague that prowls in the darkness
nor the scourge that lays waste at noon.

A thousand may fall at your side,
ten thousand fall at your right,
you, it will never approach;
God's faithfulness is buckler and shield.

Your eyes have only to look
to see how the wicked are repaid,
you who have said: "LORD, my refuge!"
and have made the Most High your dwelling.

Upon you no evil shall fall,
no plague approach where you dwell.
For you God has commanded the angels,
to keep you in all your ways.

They shall bear you upon their hands
lest you strike your foot against a stone.
On the lion and the viper you will tread
and trample the young lion and the dragon.

You set your love on me so I will save you,
protect you for you know my name.
When you call I shall answer: "I am with you,"
I will save you in distress and give you glory.

With length of days I will content you;
I shall let you see my saving power.

PSALM PRAYER

Hear our prayers, Lord Jesus,
and cover us with the wings of your cross.
Whatever the changes and chances of this
    mortal life,
may we always find strength in your
    unchanging love,
O Savior of the world and lover of humanity,

living and reigning with the Father and
the Holy Spirit,
now and for ever.
~*Amen.*

READING   *Philippians 4:8–9*

Beloved, whatever is true, whatever is
honorable, whatever is just, whatever is pure,
whatever is pleasing, whatever is commend-
able, if there is any excellence and if there
is anything worthy of praise, think about these
things. Keep on doing the things that you
have learned and received and heard and seen
in me, and the God of peace will be with you.

SILENCE

RESPONSE

Send forth your light and your truth;
~*Let these be my guide.*

CANTICLE OF THE BEATITUDES
Matthew 5:3–10

*You are the salt of the earth and the light of
the world.*

Blessed are the poor in spirit,
for theirs is the kingdom of heaven.
Blessed are those who mourn,
for they will be comforted.
Blessed are the meek,
for they will inherit the earth.
Blessed are those who hunger and thirst
    for righteousness,
for they will be filled.

Blessed are the merciful,
for they will receive mercy.
Blessed are the pure in heart,
for they will see God.
Blessed are the peacemakers,
for they will be called children of God.
Blessed are those who are persecuted for
    righteousness' sake,
for theirs is the kingdom of heaven.

Glory to God: Creator, Redeemer, and Sanctifier,
now and always and for ever and ever. Amen.

INTERCESSIONS

For a fresh outpouring of the Holy Spirit,
let us pray to the Lord.
~Lord, hear our prayer.

For zeal in the Lord's service,
~Lord, hear our prayer.

For heartfelt sympathy for all human needs,
~*Lord, hear our prayer.*

For the sick and dying in their pain and humiliation,
~*Lord, hear our prayer.*

For those who have gone before us through the gates of death,
~*Lord, hear our prayer.*

LORD'S PRAYER

CLOSING PRAYER

Lord of every time and place,
as evening falls
fill this night with your radiance.
May we sleep in peace and rise with joy
to welcome the light of a new day in your name.
We ask this through Christ our Lord.
~*Amen.*

May the God of all grace who has called us to
eternal glory in Christ **+** restore, establish and
strengthen us.
~*Amen.*

O Lord, + open my lips.
~*And my mouth shall declare your praise.*

We adore you, O Christ, and we bless you.
~*For by your holy cross you have redeemed
the world.*

HYMN

PSALM 17:1–9

*During his life on earth, Jesus prayed to his
Father and was heard.*

LORD, hear a cause that is just,
pay heed to my cry.
Turn your ear to my prayer,
no deceit is on my lips.

From you may my judgement come forth.
Your eyes discern the truth.

You search my heart, you visit me by night.
You test me and find in me no wrong.
My words are not sinful like human words.

I kept from violence because of your word,
I keep my feet firmly in your paths;
there was no faltering in my steps.

I am here and I call, you will hear me, O God.
Turn your ear to me; hear my words.
Display your great love, you whose
    right hand saves
your friends from those who rebel against them.

Guard me as the apple of your eye.
Hide me in the shadow of your wings
from the violent attack of the wicked.

PSALM PRAYER

Loving Father,
by the cross and passion of your dear Son,
you saved humanity from sin and error.
Grant that by steadfast faith in
    his sacrificial death
we may triumph in the power of
    his enduring victory,
through the same Christ Jesus our Lord.
~*Amen.*

READING *John 3:14–17*

Jesus said, "Just as Moses lifted up the serpent
in the wilderness, so must the Son-of-Man
be lifted up, that whoever believes in him may
have eternal life. For God loved the world in
this way, that God gave the Son, the only
begotten one, so that everyone who believes in
him may not perish but may have eternal life.

Indeed, God did not send the Son into the world to condemn the world, but in order that the world might be saved through him."

SILENCE

RESPONSE

Christ is victor, Christ is ruler.
~*Christ is Lord of all.*

CANTICLE OF THE SUFFERING SERVANT OF GOD   *Isaiah 53:11b, 2–3b, 4–6*

Jesus is now crowned with glory and honor because of the death he suffered.

The righteous one, my servant,
shall make many righteous,
and he shall bear their iniquities.

He grew up before the LORD
like a young plant,
and like a root out of dry ground;
he had no form or majesty
that we should look at him,
nothing in his appearance
that we should desire him.
He was despised and rejected by others;
a man of suffering
and acquainted with infirmity.

Surely he has borne our infirmities
and carried our diseases;
yet we accounted him stricken,
struck down by God,
and afflicted.

He was wounded
for our transgressions,
crushed for our iniquities;
upon him was the punishment
that made us whole,
and by his bruises
we are healed.

All we like sheep have gone astray;
we have all turned to our own way,
and the LORD has laid on him
the iniquity of us all.

Glory to the Father, and to the Son,
and to the Holy Spirit:
as it was in the beginning, is now,
and will be for ever. Amen.

LORD'S PRAYER

CLOSING PRAYER

God of mercy and compassion,
long-suffering in the face of our wickedness,
blot out our sins by the power of the cross

and keep our lives free from deadly sin
by the grace of your Holy Spirit,
through Christ Jesus, our blessed Savior.
~Amen.

May the glorious passion of our Lord Jesus
Christ **+** bring us to the joys of paradise.
~Amen.

FRIDAY EVENING

Jesus Christ **+** is the light of the world.
~A light no darkness can extinguish.

HYMN

PSALM 31:1–6, 19–20

Into your hands, O Lord, I commend my spirit.

In you, O LORD, I take refuge.
Let me never be put to shame.
In your justice, set me free,
hear me and speedily rescue me.

Be a rock of refuge for me,
a mighty stronghold to save me,
for you are my rock, my stronghold.
For your name's sake, lead me and guide me.

Release me from the snares they have hidden
for you are my refuge, Lord.
Into your hands I commend my spirit.
It is you who will redeem me, LORD.

How great is the goodness, LORD,
that you keep for those who fear you,
that you show to those who trust you
in the sight of all.

PSALM PRAYER

Lord Jesus Christ,
by your cross blot out our sins
and increase our holiness.
Sustain the living,
give eternal rest to the dead
and bring everyone to the house of life,
where we will praise, thank and glorify
the Father, the Son, and the Holy Spirit,
for ever and ever.
~*Amen.*

READING   *Mark 8:34–36*

Jesus said to his disciples: "If any want to
become my followers, let them deny themselves
and take up their cross and follow me. For
those who want to save their life will lose it, and
those who lose their life for my sake, and for
the sake of the gospel, will save it. For what will

it profit them to gain the whole world and forfeit their life?"

SILENCE

RESPONSE

Let us glory in the cross of our Lord
Jesus Christ,
~*In him is our salvation, life and resurrection.*

CANTICLE OF THE HOLY CROSS
1 Peter 2:21–24

> *By the power of your holy cross, O Savior,
> save us.*

Christ suffered for you,
leaving you an example,
so that you should follow in his steps.

"He committed no sin,
and no deceit
was found in his mouth."

When he was abused,
he did not return abuse;
when he suffered,
he did not threaten;
but entrusted himself
to the one who judges justly.

He himself bore our sins
in his body on the cross,
so that, free from sins,
we might live for righteousness;
by his wounds
we have been healed.

To the King of the ages, immortal, invisible,
    the only wise God,
be honor and glory, through Jesus Christ,
for ever and ever. Amen.

INTERCESSIONS

With travelers lost in a parched and burning
desert:
~*We cry unto you, O Lord.*

With people shipwrecked on a lonely coast:
~*We cry unto you, O Lord.*

With a mother robbed of bread for her
starving children:
~*We cry unto you, O Lord.*

With a prisoner unjustly confined to a dank
prison:
~*We cry unto you, O Lord.*

With a slave torn by the master's lash:
~*We cry unto you, O Lord.*

With an innocent person led to execution:
~*We cry unto you, O Lord.*

With Christ on the cross when he cried out: "My God, my God, why have you forsaken me?"
~*We cry unto you, O Lord.*

LORD'S PRAYER

CLOSING PRAYER

Lord Jesus Christ, Son of the living God,
at the evening hour you rested in the sepulchre,
and sanctified the grave to be a bed of hope for
   your people.
Make us so repentant for our sins,
which were the cause of your passion,
that when our bodies lie in the dust,
our souls may live with you,
for ever and ever.
~*Amen.*

May the glorious passion of our Lord Jesus Christ + bring us to the joys of paradise.
~*Amen.*

O Lord, **+** open my lips.
~*And my mouth shall declare your praise.*

Blest be the Lord our God, the ruler of
the universe.
~*Now and always and for ever and ever.*

HYMN

PSALM 92:2–6, 13–16

It is good to proclaim your love in the morning.

It is good to give thanks to the LORD,
to make music to your name, O Most High,
to proclaim your love in the morning
and your truth in the watches of the night,
on the ten-stringed lyre and the lute,
with the murmuring sound of the harp.

Your deeds, O LORD, have made me glad;
for the work of your hands I shout for joy.
O LORD, how great are your works!
How deep are your designs!

The just will flourish like the palm tree
and grow like a Lebanon cedar.
Planted in the house of the LORD
they will flourish in the courts of our God,
still bearing fruit when they are old,
still full of sap, still green,
to proclaim that the LORD is just.
My rock, in whom there is no wrong.

PSALM PRAYER

Just and merciful God,
we marvel at your faithfulness
and at your great deeds on our behalf.
Help us to love and thank you
every day of our lives
and become like palm trees,
green and heavy with fruit
even in old age.
In Jesus' name.
~Amen.

READING   *Deuteronomy 6:4–7*

Hear, O Israel: The LORD is our God, the
LORD alone. You shall love the LORD your
God with all your heart, and with all your soul,
and with all your might. Keep these words
that I am commanding you today in your heart.
Recite them to your children and talk about

them when you are at home and when you are
away, when you lie down and when you rise.

SILENCE

RESPONSE
In you is the source of life.
~*And in your light we see light.*

CANTICLE OF ISAIAH   *Isaiah 26:1–4, 7–8*
O dwellers in the dust, awake and sing for joy!

We have a strong city;
the LORD sets up victory
like walls and bulwarks.

Open the gates,
so that the righteous nation that keeps faith
may enter in.

Those of steadfast mind you keep in peace—
in peace because they trust in you.

Trust in the LORD forever,
for in the LORD GOD
you have an everlasting rock.

The way of the righteous is level;
O Just One, you make smooth the path
    of the righteous.
In the path of your judgments,
O LORD, we wait for you;
your name and your renown
are the soul's desire.

To the King of the ages, immortal, invisible,
the only wise God,
be honor and glory, through Jesus Christ,
for ever and ever. Amen.

LORD'S PRAYER

CLOSING PRAYER

Abba, heavenly Father,
in you we live and move and have our being.
Guide and govern us by your Holy Spirit
so that we may never forget you
during all the cares and occupations of life,
but recall each morning
that we are always walking in your sight,
through Christ Jesus, our Lord and Savior.
~*Amen.*

May the Word made flesh, full of grace and
truth, **+** bless us and keep us.
~*Amen.*

The scriptures lie ever more clearly open to us. They are revealed, heart and sinew. The meaning of the words comes through to us not just by way of commentaries but by what we ourselves have gone through. Seized of the identical feelings in which the psalm was composed or sung we become, as it were, its author.

~John Cassian, ca. 365–435

THIRD WEEK

I am + the light of the world.
~*Whoever follows me will walk in my light.*

HYMN

PSALM 113:1-8

God pulls down tyrants from their thrones and raises up the lowly.

Praise, O servants of the LORD,
praise the name of the LORD!
May the name of the LORD be blessed
both now and for evermore!
From the rising of the sun to its setting
praised be the name of the LORD!

High above all nations is the Lord,
above the heavens God's glory.
Who is like the LORD, our God,
the one enthroned on high,
who stoops from the heights to look down,
to look down upon heaven and earth?

From the dust God lifts up the lowly,
from the dungheap God raises the poor
to set them in the company of rulers,
yes, with the rulers of the people.

PSALM PRAYER

Bountiful God,
your name is praised from sunrise to sunset
in every quarter of the world.
Bend down to see the poor and needy
and rescue them from the dust and mire
so that they may honor and glorify you
from east to west and from pole to pole,
through all the ages of ages.
~*Amen.*

READING   *1 Peter 5:6–9a*

Sisters and brothers, humble yourselves under
the mighty hand of God, so that he may
exalt you in due time. Cast all your anxiety
on him, because he cares for you. Discipline
yourselves, keep alert. Like a roaring lion

your adversary the devil prowls around,
looking for someone to devour. Resist him,
steadfast in your faith.

SILENCE

RESPONSE

Let my prayer arise before you like incense,
~*The raising of my hands like an evening
oblation.*

CANTICLE OF THE WORD
John 1:1–5, 10–14

> *All things have been created through Christ and
> for Christ.*

In the beginning was the Word,
and the Word was with God,
and the Word was God.
He was in the beginning with God.

All things came into being through him,
and without him not one thing came into being.
What has come into being in him was life,
and the life was the light of all people.
The light shines in the darkness,
and the darkness did not overcome it.

He was in the world,
and the world came into being through him;
yet the world did not know him.
He came to what was his own,
and his own people did not accept him.

But to all who received him,
who believed in his name,
he gave power to become children of God,
who were born,
not of blood or of the will of the flesh
or of the will of man,
but of God.

And the Word became flesh
and lived among us,
and we have seen his glory,
the glory as of a father's only son,
full of grace and truth.

Glory to the Father, and to the Son,
and to the Holy Spirit:
as it was in the beginning, is now,
and will be for ever. Amen.

APOSTLES' CREED

INTERCESSIONS

Lord Christ, living stone, rejected by your own
people but chosen by God:
~*Hear our prayers.*

Lord Christ, put to death in the flesh,
raised to life in the Spirit:
~*Hear our prayers.*

Lord Christ, Lamb of God without spot or stain:
~*Hear our prayers.*

Lord Christ, shepherd and guardian of our souls:
~*Hear our prayers.*

Lord Christ, seated at the Father's right hand
in glory:
~*Hear our prayers.*

Lord Christ, whose kingdom shall have no end:
~*Hear our prayers.*

LORD'S PRAYER

Let us pray as Jesus taught us:
~*Our Father . . .*

CLOSING PRAYER

Almighty and everlasting God,
by the bitter death of your dear Son,
and by his glorious rising again,
you have redeemed humanity.
In the joy of his risen life,

may we die daily to sin and error
and live for ever in Christ our Savior.
~*Amen.*

May the Word made flesh, full of grace and
truth, **+** bless us and keep us.
~*Amen.*

SUNDAY MORNING

O Lord, **+** open my lips.
~*And my mouth shall declare your praise.*

This is the day the Lord has made! Alleluia!
~*Let us rejoice and be glad! Alleluia!*

HYMN

PSALM 47

Christ's kingdom will have no end! Alleluia!

All peoples, clap your hands,
cry to God with shouts of joy!
For the LORD, the Most High, we must fear,
great king over all the earth.

God subdues peoples under us
and nations under our feet.
Our inheritance, our glory, is from God,
given to Jacob out of love.

God goes up with shouts of joy;
the Lord goes up with trumpet blast.
Sing praise for God, sing praise,
sing praise to our king, sing praise.

God is king of all the earth,
sing praise with all your skill.
God is king over the nations;
God reigns enthroned in holiness.

The leaders of the people are assembled
with the people of Abraham's God.
The rulers of the earth belong to God,
to God who reigns over all.

PSALM PRAYER

Abba, dear Father,
you willed to restore all things
in your beloved Son,
the ruler of all the earth.
Heal the divisions of nations and peoples
caused by the discord of sin,
and subject us to the gracious rule of him

who lives with you and the Holy Spirit,
one God, now and for ever.
~*Amen.*

READING   *1 Corinthians 15:3–8*

Brothers and sisters, I handed on to you as of
first importance what I in turn had received:
that Christ died for our sins in accordance with
the scriptures, and that he was buried, and that
he was raised on the third day in accordance
with the scriptures, and that he appeared to
Cephas, then to the twelve. Then he appeared
to more than five hundred brothers and sisters
at one time, most of whom are still alive,
though some have died. Then he appeared to
James, then to all the apostles. Last of all, as to
one untimely born, he appeared also to me.

SILENCE

RESPONSE

Arise, O Christ, and help us.
~*And deliver us for your name's sake.*

CANTICLE OF THE CHURCH

We praise you, O God,
we acclaim you as Lord;
all creation worships you,
the Father everlasting.
To you all angels, all the powers of heaven,
cherubim and seraphim, sing in endless praise:

Holy, holy, holy Lord, God of power and might,
heaven and earth are full of your glory.

The glorious company of apostles praise you.
The noble fellowship of prophets praise you.
The white-robed army of martyrs praise you.
Throughout the world the holy Church
    acclaims you:

Father, of majesty unbounded,
your true and only Son, worthy of all praise,
the Holy Spirit, advocate and guide.

You, Christ, are the king of glory,
the eternal Son of the Father.
When you took our flesh to set us free
you humbly chose the Virgin's womb.
You overcame the sting of death,
and opened the kingdom of heaven
    to all believers.
You are seated at God's right hand in glory.
We believe that you will come to be our judge.

Come then, Lord, and help your people,
bought with the price of your own blood,
and bring us with your saints
to glory everlasting.

APOSTLES' CREED

LORD'S PRAYER

Let us pray as Jesus taught us:
~*Our Father . . .*

CLOSING PRAYER

Lord Jesus Christ,
by your holy cross and glorious resurrection,
you dealt death a deathblow
and brought life to those in the grave.
May your blessed passion
be the joy of the whole world
and the glory of your rising from the tomb
always be our song,
O Savior of the world,
living and reigning
with the Father and the Holy Spirit,
now and for ever.
~*Amen.*

Peace be with the whole community, and love
with faith, from God the Father **+** and the
Lord Jesus Christ.
~*Amen.*

Light and peace **+** in Jesus Christ our Lord.
~*Thanks be to God.*

HYMN

PSALM 85:9-14

Salvation is near! Alleluia! Glory is filling our land! Alleluia!

I will hear what the LORD has to say,
a voice that speaks of peace,
peace for his people and friends
and those who turn to God in their hearts.
Salvation is near for the God-fearing,
and his glory will dwell in our land.

Mercy and faithfulness have met;
justice and peace have embraced.
Faithfulness shall spring from the earth
and justice look down from heaven.

The LORD will make us prosper
and our earth shall yield its fruit.
Justice shall march in the forefront,
and peace shall follow the way.

PSALM PRAYER

Risen Lord and Savior,
give us true hearts
that work for justice and peace
everywhere and at all times.
Fill our land with the glory of the age to come
and refresh us with the love and fidelity
that mark the Good News of the gospel.
You live and reign now and forever.
~*Amen.*

READING   *1 Corinthians 15:20–23*

Sisters and brothers, Christ has been raised
from the dead, the first fruits of those who have
died. For since death came through a human
being, the resurrection of the dead has also
come through a human being; for as all die in
Adam, so all will be made alive in Christ. But
each in his own order: Christ the first fruits,
then at his coming those who belong to Christ.

SILENCE

RESPONSE

By the wood of the cross! Alleluia!
~*Joy came into the whole world! Alleluia!*

CANTICLE OF MARY   *Luke 1:46–55*

Rejoice, O Queen of heaven! Alleluia! for the
Son you bore! Alleluia! has arisen as he promised!
Alleluia! Pray for us to God the Father! Alleluia!

My soul **+** proclaims the greatness of the Lord.
My spirit sings to God, my saving God,
Who on this day above all others favored me
And raised me up, a light for all to see.

Through me great deeds will God make
   manifest,
And all the earth will come to call me blest.
Unbounded love and mercy sure will I proclaim
For all who know and praise God's holy name.

God's mighty arm, protector of the just,
Will guard the weak and raise them
   from the dust.
But mighty kings will swiftly fall
   from thrones corrupt.
The strong brought low, the lowly lifted up.

Soon will the poor and hungry of the earth
Be richly blest, be given greater worth.
And Israel, as once foretold to Abraham,
Will live in peace throughout the promised land.

All glory be to God, Creator blest,
To Jesus Christ, God's love made manifest,
And to the Holy Spirit, gentle Comforter,
All glory be, both now and evermore. Amen.

INTERCESSIONS

Save your people, Lord, and bless
your inheritance.
~*Govern and uphold them now and always.*

Day by day we bless you.
~*We praise your name for ever.*

Keep us today, Lord, from all sin.
~*Have mercy on us, Lord, have mercy.*

Lord, show us your love and mercy,
~*for we put our trust in you.*

In you, Lord, is our hope:
~*let us never be put to shame.*

LORD'S PRAYER

CLOSING PRAYER

Lord Jesus Christ,
in your suffering on Golgotha
you cried out to your dear Father
and he delivered you out of death.
By the power of your holy cross,
rescue us from the abyss of sin,
renew this world of yours

and flood our minds with the light
of your glorious resurrection,
O Savior of the world,
living and reigning for ever and ever.
~*Amen.*

Peace be with the whole community, and love
with faith, from God the Father **+** and the
Lord Jesus Christ.
~*Amen.*

MONDAY MORNING

O Lord, **+** open my lips.
~*And my mouth shall declare your praise.*

Come, let us adore the true God,
One in Three and Three in One.
~*Come, let us adore the living God.*

HYMN

PSALM 95:1–7; 99:9

Let us worship the Lord in the beauty of holiness.

Come, ring out our joy to the LORD;
hail the rock who saves us.
Let us come before God, giving thanks,
with songs let us hail the Lord.

A mighty God is the LORD,
a great king above all gods,
in whose hands are the depths of the earth;
the heights of the mountains as well.
The sea belongs to God, who made it
and the dry land shaped by his hands.

Come in; let us bow and bend low;
let us kneel before the God who made us
for this is our God and we
the people who belong to his pasture,
the flock that is led by his hand.

Exalt the LORD our God;
bow down before God's holy mountain
for the LORD our God is holy.

PSALM PRAYER

Good Shepherd of your people,
Lord of all the powers that be,
as we worship before you
in the beauty of holiness,
feed us with the bread of life
and teach us to praise you
always and for everything,
in and through Christ our Lord.
~*Amen.*

READING   *1 Peter 1:13–16*

Sisters and brothers, prepare your minds for
action; discipline yourselves; set all your
hope on the grace that Jesus Christ will bring
you when he is revealed. Like obedient
children, do not be conformed to the desires
that you formerly had in ignorance. Instead,
as he who called you is holy, be holy yourselves
in all your conduct; for it is written, "You
shall be holy, for I am holy."

SILENCE

RESPONSE

Show us your mercy, Lord God Almighty.
~And we will be saved!

CANTICLE OF WISDOM
Wisdom 16:20–21, 24, 26b

*You created the universe, O Lord; it is
at your command.*

You gave your people the food of angels.
From heaven you sent down bread
that was ready to eat,
and they did not have to prepare it.

The food you gave delighted everyone,
no matter what his taste.
All this showed how lovingly
you care for your children.

The food satisfied the desire
of everyone who ate it;
it was changed to suit each person's taste.

You created the universe;
it is at your command.
It is your word that maintains those
who put their trust in you.

Glory to you, Source of all being,
Eternal Word, and Holy Spirit:
as it was in the beginning, is now,
and will be for ever. Amen.

LORD'S PRAYER

CLOSING PRAYER

God of peace,
you brought back from the dead
the great Shepherd of the flock,
our Lord Jesus Christ.
By the blood of the new and everlasting
    covenant,
provide us with everything we need
    for doing your will

---

so that we may please you in all our actions,
through the same Christ our Lord,
to whom be glory for ever and ever.
~*Amen.*

May the God of peace sanctify us wholly,
and may our spirit, soul and body **+** be kept
sound and blameless at the coming of our
Lord Jesus Christ.
~*Amen.*

MONDAY EVENING

Jesus Christ **+** is the light of the world.
~*A light no darkness can extinguish.*

HYMN

PSALM 119:105–112

Your word is a light for my path.

Your word is a lamp for my steps
and a light for my path.
I have sworn and made up my mind
to obey your decrees.

LORD, I am deeply afflicted;
by your word give me life.
Accept, LORD, the homage of my lips
and teach me your decrees.

Though I carry my life in my hands,
I remember your law.
Though the wicked try to ensnare me,
I do not stray from your precepts.

Your will is my heritage for ever,
the joy of my heart.
I set myself to carry out your statutes
in fullness, for ever.

PSALM PRAYER

Creator of night and day,
may your divine word be
a lamp for our feet
and a light for our path.
As children of the light,
may we walk in the sure ways
of your sacred teaching
all the days of our life.
To you be the glory for ever and ever.
~*Amen.*

READING   *1 John 1:1–3*

Brothers and sisters, we declare to you what was
from the beginning, what we have heard, what
we have seen with our eyes, what we have
looked at and touched with our hands, concern-
ing the word of life—this life was revealed, and
we have seen it and testify to it, and declare to
you the eternal life that was with the Father and
was revealed to us—we declare to you what
we have seen and heard so that you also may
have communion with us; and truly our communion is with the Father and with Jesus Christ,
the Son.

SILENCE

RESPONSE

In times of trouble I pray to the Lord.
~All night long I lift my hands in prayer.

CANTICLE OF A JOYFUL ASSEMBLY
Hebrews 12:22–24a, 28–29

We come to the city of the living God.

We have come to Mount Zion
and to the city of the living God,
the heavenly Jerusalem,
and to innumerable angels in festal gathering.

And to the assembly of the firstborn
who are enrolled in heaven,
and to God the judge of all,
and to the spirits of the righteous made perfect,
and to Jesus, the mediator of a new covenant.

Since we are receiving a kingdom
that cannot be shaken,
let us give thanks,
by which we offer to God an acceptable worship
with reverence and awe;
for indeed our God is a consuming fire.

Glory to God: Creator, Redeemer, and Sanctifier,
now and always and for ever and ever. Amen.

INTERCESSIONS

For the dawn of truth to light the church,
let us pray to the Lord,
~*Lord, hear our prayer.*

For the fire of Christ's love to warm the world,
~*Lord, hear our prayer.*

For a fresh outpouring of the gifts of the Spirit,
~*Lord, hear our prayer.*

For the conversion of all who do not believe,
~*Lord, hear our prayer.*

For the healing of human hatred and discord,
~*Lord, hear our prayer.*

LORD'S PRAYER

CLOSING PRAYER

Lord Jesus, our Savior,
as evening returns and night falls,
may the sun of your saving presence
go on shining in our hearts,
and put to flight the threatening gloom
of sin and danger.
You live and reign now and for ever.
~*Amen.*

May the God of hope fill us with all joy and
peace in believing so that by the power of the
Holy Spirit **+** we may abound in hope.
~*Amen.*

TUESDAY MORNING

O Lord, **+** open my lips.
~*And my mouth shall declare your praise.*

Blest be the Father, the Word, and the Spirit.
~*For these Three are One.*

HYMN

PSALM 96

God reigns from the tree of the cross.

O sing a new song to the LORD,
sing to the LORD all the earth.
O sing to the LORD, bless his name.

Proclaim God's help day by day,
tell among the nations his glory
and his wonders among all the peoples.

The LORD is great and worthy of praise,
to be feared above all gods;
the gods of the heathen are naught.

It was the LORD who made the heavens.
His are majesty and honor and power
and splendor in the holy place.

Give the LORD, you families of peoples,
give the LORD glory and power;
give the LORD the glory of his name.

Bring an offering and enter God's courts,
worship the LORD in the temple.
O earth, stand in fear of the LORD.

Proclaim to the nations: "God is king."
The world was made firm in its place;
God will judge the people in fairness.

Let the heavens rejoice and the earth be glad,
let the sea and all that is in it thunder praise,
let the land and all it bears rejoice,
all the trees of the wood shout for joy

at the presence of the LORD who comes,
who comes to rule the earth,
comes with justice to rule the world,
and to judge the peoples with truth.

PSALM PRAYER

Wonderful and glorious God,
all creation sings your praise
because you fill the world with vibrant life.
May the sweet sovereignty of Christ
who rules from the cross
be our hope and confidence
as we tremble in your awesome presence.
We ask this through the same Christ our Lord.
~*Amen.*

READING   *1 Peter 1:17–21*

Sisters and brothers, if you invoke as Father
the one who judges all people impartially
according to their deeds, live in reverent fear
during the time of your exile. You know that
you were ransomed from the futile ways
inherited from your ancestors, not with perishable things like silver or gold, but with the

precious blood of Christ, like that of a lamb
without defect or blemish. He was destined
before the foundation of the world, but
was revealed at the end of the ages for your
sake. Through him you have come to trust
in God, who raised him from the dead and gave
him glory, so that your faith and hope are set
on God.

SILENCE

RESPONSE

How good it is to sing in your honor.
~*To proclaim your constant love every morning.*

CANTICLE OF WISDOM
Sirach 14:20–27; 15:3–6

Great is the wisdom of the Lord!

It is a happy person
who is concerned with Wisdom
and who uses good sense.
Anyone who studies the ways of Wisdom
will also learn her secrets.

Go after Wisdom like a hunter
looking for game.
Look into her windows
and listen at her doors.

Camp as close to her house
as you can get,
and you will have a fine place to live.
Build your home there,
safe beneath her protecting branches,
and shaded from the heat.

She will give you wisdom and knowledge
like food and drink.
Rely on her for support,
and you will never know the disgrace of failure.

She will make you more honored
than all your neighbors;
when you speak in the assembly,
she will give you the right words.

You will find happiness and genuine joy;
your name will be remembered forever.

To the King of ages, immortal, invisible,
the only wise God,
be honor and glory, through Jesus Christ,
for ever and ever. Amen.

LORD'S PRAYER

CLOSING PRAYER

True Light and source of all light,
dislodge all vicious tendencies from our hearts

and make us bright with virtue's light,
through Christ our Lord.
~*Amen.*

May the God of peace sanctify us, and
may our spirit, soul and body **+** be kept
sound and blameless at the coming of
our Lord Jesus Christ.
~*Amen.*

TUESDAY EVENING

The Word **+** was the source of life.
~*And this life brought light to all.*

HYMN

PSALM 121

Watch and pray in the time of trial.

I lift up my eyes to the mountains;
from where shall come my help?
My help shall come from the LORD
who made heaven and earth.

May God never allow you to stumble!
Let your guard not sleep.
Behold, neither sleeping nor slumbering,
Israel's guard.

The LORD is your guard and your shade;
and stands at your right.
By day the sun shall not smite you
nor the moon in the night.

The LORD will guard you from evil,
and will guard your soul.
The LORD will guard your going and coming
both now and for ever.

PSALM PRAYER

Lord God, our protector,
unsleeping guardian of those who look to you,
defend us by day and by night
from the stumbling blocks
of the world, the flesh and the devil,
through Jesus, our blessed Savior.
~*Amen.*

READING   *1 John 1:5a–7*

Brothers and sisters, God is light and in him
there is no darkness at all. If we say that
we have communion with God while we are
walking in darkness, we lie and do not do

what is true; but if we walk in the light as God is in the light, we have communion with one another, and the blood of Jesus, God's Son, cleanses us from all sin.

SILENCE

RESPONSE

Salvation is coming near.
~*Glory is filling our land.*

CANTICLE OF A NEW HEAVEN AND A NEW EARTH   *Revelation 21:1–2, 22–25*

The Lord God will be their light and they will reign for ever and ever.

I saw a new heaven and a new earth;
for the first heaven and the first earth
had passed away,
and the sea was no more.

I saw the holy city, the new Jerusalem,
coming down out of heaven from God,
prepared as a bride adorned for her husband.

I saw no temple in the city,
for its temple is the Lord God the Almighty
and the Lamb.

The city has no need of sun or moon
to shine on it,
for the glory of God is its light,
and its lamp is the Lamb.

The nations will walk by its light,
and the rulers of the earth
will bring their glory into it.
Its gates will never be shut by day
—and there will be no night there.

Glory to the Father, and to the Son,
and to the Holy Spirit:
as it was in the beginning, is now,
and will be for ever. Amen.

INTERCESSIONS

For the one, holy, catholic, and apostolic church,
let us pray to the Lord.
~*Lord, have mercy.*

For faithful ministers of Christ's word
and sacraments,
~*Lord, have mercy.*

For courage to do God's will in all things,
~*Lord, have mercy.*

For continual growth in God's love and service,
~*Lord, have mercy.*

For grace to walk in the footsteps of the saints,
~*Lord, have mercy.*

LORD'S PRAYER

CLOSING PRAYER

Night and day belong to you, O Lord.
May Christ, the sun of righteousness,
continue to shine in our hearts
and put to flight all evil impulses,
through the same Christ our Lord.
~*Amen.*

May the God of peace sanctify us, and
may our spirit, soul and body **+** be kept
sound and blameless at the coming of
our Lord Jesus Christ.
~*Amen.*

WEDNESDAY MORNING

O Lord, **+** open my lips.
~*And my mouth shall declare your praise.*

Blest are you, Lord.
~*God of our ancestors.*

HYMN

PSALM 97

Give glory to God's holy name!

The LORD is king, let earth rejoice,
let all the coastlands be glad.
Surrounded by cloud and darkness;
justice and right, God's throne.

A fire prepares the way;
it burns up foes on every side.
God's lightnings light up the world,
the earth trembles at the sight.

The mountains melt like wax
before the LORD of all the earth.
The skies proclaim God's justice;
all peoples see God's glory.

Let those who serve idols be ashamed,
those who boast of their worthless gods.
All you spirits worship the Lord.

Zion hears and is glad;
the people of Judah rejoice
because of your judgments, O LORD.

For you indeed are the LORD
most high above all the earth,
exalted far above all spirits.

The LORD loves those who hate evil,
guards the souls of the saints,
and sets them free from the wicked.

Light shines forth for the just
and joy for the upright of heart.
Rejoice, you just, in the LORD;
give glory to God's holy name.

PSALM PRAYER

Great and glorious God,
your awesome majesty puts fear
in those who worship the idols
of money and power.
Shield our lives from falsity
and rain down the light of discernment
on the people of faith,
in Jesus' name.
~Amen.

READING   *1 Peter 1:22–23, 25b*

Brothers and sisters, now that you have purified
your souls by your obedience to the truth so
that you have genuine mutual love, love one
another deeply from the heart. You have been
born anew, not of perishable but of imperishable seed, through the living and enduring word
of God. That word is the good news that was
announced to you.

You are my God.
~*I pray to you all day long.*

CANTICLE OF GOD'S CHILDREN
Sirach 36:1–7, 21–22

Have mercy, O Lord, on the people called by
your name.

Have mercy upon us, O God of all,
and put all the nations in fear of you.
Lift up your hand against foreign nations
and let them see your might.

As you have used us to show your holiness
  to them,
so use them to show your glory to us.
Then they will know, as we have known,
that there is no God but you, O Lord.

Give new signs and work other wonders;
make your hand and your right arm glorious.
Reward those who wait for you
and let your prophets be found trustworthy.

Hear, O Lord, the prayer of your servants,
according to your goodwill toward your people,
and all who are on earth will know
that you are the Lord, the God of the ages.

Glory to you, Source of all being,
Eternal Word, and Holy Spirit:
as it was in the beginning, is now,
and will be for ever. Amen.

LORD'S PRAYER

CLOSING PRAYER

Heavenly Father of Jesus,
all you do is for our good,
and your commandments
are the life of the world,
teaching us what is right and holy.
Bless and sanctify your people,
fill us with awe of your holy name
and enable us to praise you worthily,
through Jesus Christ our Lord.
~*Amen.*

May the Lord + direct our hearts in the love of
God and the patience of Christ.
~*Amen.*

WEDNESDAY EVENING

The Word + was the source of life.
~*And this life brought light to all.*

HYMN

PSALM 122

You have come to the city of the living God, the heavenly Jerusalem.

I rejoiced when I heard them say:
"Let us go to God's house."
And now our feet are standing
within your gates, O Jerusalem.

Jerusalem is built as a city
strongly compact.
It is there that the tribes go up,
the tribes of the LORD.

For Israel's law it is,
there to praise the LORD's name.
There were set the thrones of judgement
of the house of David.

For the peace of Jerusalem pray:
"Peace be to your homes!
May peace reign in your walls,
in your palaces, peace!"

For love of my family and friends
I say: "Peace upon you."
For love of the house of the LORD
I will ask for your good.

PSALM PRAYER

Founder of Jerusalem, the city of peace,
and builder of the heavenly Jerusalem,
be the joy and delight of all those
who live in your holy church
and long for its reform and renewal.
We ask this through Christ our Lord.
~*Amen.*

READING   *1 John 2:3 – 6*

Sisters and brothers, By this we may be sure
that we know God, if we obey his commandments. Whoever says, "I have come to know
him," but does not obey his commandments, is
a liar, and in such a person the truth does not
exist; but whoever obeys his word, truly in this
person the love of God has reached perfection.
By this we may be sure that we are in him:
whoever says, "I abide in him," ought to walk
just as Jesus walked.

SILENCE

RESPONSE

Lord God my Savior, I cry out all day.
~*And at night I come before you.*

CANTICLE OF SAINT FRANCIS FOR BROTHER SUN AND SISTER MOON

Most high, Almighty, good Lord!
All praise, glory, honor and exaltation are yours!
To you alone do they belong,
and no mere mortal dares pronounce your name.
We praise you, O Lord!

Praise to you, O Lord our God, for all
    your creatures:
first, for our dear Brother Sun,
who gives us the day
and illumines us with his light;
fair is he, in splendor radiant,
bearing your very likeness, O Lord.
We praise you, O Lord!

For our Sister Moon,
and for the bright, shining stars:
We praise you, O Lord!

For our Brother Wind,
for fair and stormy seasons
and all heaven's varied moods,
by which you nourish all that you have made:
We praise you, O Lord!

For our Sister Water,
so useful, lowly, precious and pure.
We praise you, O Lord!

For our Brother Fire,
who brightens up our darkest nights:
beautiful is he and eager,
invincible and keen:
We praise you, O Lord!

For our Mother Earth,
who sustains and feeds us,
producing fair fruits,
and many-colored flowers and herbs:
We praise you, O Lord!

For those who forgive one another
    for love of you,
and who patiently bear sickness and other trials.
Happy are they who peacefully endure;
you will crown them, O Most High!
We praise you, O Lord!

For our Sister Death,
the inescapable fact of life.
Woe to those who die in mortal sin!
Happy are those she finds doing your will!
From the Second Death they stand immune:
We praise you, O Lord!

All creatures,
praise and glorify my Lord
and give him thanks
and serve him in great humility:
We praise you, O Lord!

INTERCESSIONS

O God, hear my cry!
~*Listen to my prayer!*

From the end of the earth I call.
~*My heart is faint.*

Let me dwell in your tent for ever.
~*And hide in the shelter of your wings.*

For you, O God, hear my prayer.
~*Grant me the heritage of those who fear you.*

I will always praise your name.
~*And day after day fulfill my vows.*

LORD'S PRAYER

CLOSING PRAYER

Father of us all,
in your mercy hear our evening prayer,
that freed from all sin and danger
we may always walk in your light,
through Jesus Christ our Lord.
~*Amen.*

May the Lord **+** direct our hearts in the love of
God and the patience of Christ.
~*Amen.*

O Lord, **+** open my lips.
~*And my mouth shall declare your praise.*

Holy is God, holy and strong.
~*Holy and living for ever.*

HYMN

PSALM 98

Christ will come again in glory to judge the living and the dead.

Sing a new song to the LORD
who has worked wonders;
whose right hand and holy arm
have brought salvation.

The LORD has made known salvation;
has shown justice to the nations;
has remembered truth and love
for the house of Israel.

All the ends of the earth have seen
the salvation of our God.
Shout to the LORD, all the earth,
ring out your joy.

Sing psalms to the LORD with the harp
with the sound of music.
With trumpets and the sound of the horn
acclaim the King, the LORD.

Let the sea and all within it, thunder;
the world, and all its peoples.
Let the rivers clap their hands
and the hills ring out their joy

at the presence of the LORD, who comes,
who comes to rule the earth.
God will rule the world with justice
and the peoples with fairness.

PSALM PRAYER

Lord of wonderful deeds,
as the day of Christ Jesus draws near,
bring to completion the good work
that you have begun in us.
Make us pure and blameless in your sight,
and prepare us for the day of Christ
when he comes to rule the world.
He lives and reigns with you and the Holy Spirit,
now and for ever.
~*Amen.*

READING   *1 Peter 2:2–5*

Brothers and sisters, like newborn infants,
long for the pure, spiritual milk, so that by it
you may grow into salvation—if indeed you
have tasted that the Lord is good. Come to the
Lord, a living stone, though rejected by mortals
yet chosen and precious in God's sight, and
like living stones, let yourselves be built into a
spiritual house, to be a holy priesthood, to offer
spiritual sacrifices acceptable to God through
Jesus Christ.

SILENCE

RESPONSE

How happy are the people who worship you
with songs.
~*Who live in the light of your kindness.*

CANTICLE OF ISAIAH   *Isaiah 2:2–5*

Come, let us walk in the light of the Lord!

In days to come
the mountain of the LORD's house
shall be established as the highest of the
    mountains,
and shall be raised above the hills;
all the nations shall stream to it.

Many peoples shall come and say,
"Come, let us go up to the mountain
   of the LORD,
to the house of Jacob's God,
who will teach us the ways of God,
that we may walk the paths of the LORD."

For out of Zion shall go forth instruction,
and the word of the LORD from Jerusalem.
God shall judge between the nations,
and shall arbitrate for many peoples;
they shall beat their swords into plowshares,
and their spears into pruning hooks;
nation shall not lift up sword against nation,
neither shall they learn war any more.

Glory to the Father, and to the Son,
and to the Holy Spirit:
as it was in the beginning, is now,
and will be for ever. Amen.

LORD'S PRAYER

CLOSING PRAYER

Lord God, ruler of heaven and earth,
direct and sanctify, rule and guide
our hearts and bodies,
our thoughts, words and deeds
to respect your law and keep your
   commandments,

so that today and every day
we may be kept safe and free,
O Savior of the world,
living and reigning for ever and ever.
~Amen.

May the God of all grace who has called us to
eternal glory in Christ + restore, establish and
strengthen us.
~Amen.

THURSDAY EVENING

I am + the light of the world.
~That shines on all people.

HYMN

PSALM 124

*Our help comes from the Lord, who made
heaven and earth.*

"If the LORD had not been on our side,"
this is Israel's song.
"If the LORD had not been on our side
when they rose up against us,
then would they have swallowed us alive
when their anger was kindled.

Then would the waters have engulfed us,
the torrent gone over us;
over our head would have swept
the raging waters."

Blessed be the LORD who did not give us
a prey to their teeth!
Our life, like a bird, has escaped
from the snare of the fowler.

Indeed the snare has been broken
and we have escaped.
Our help is in the name of the LORD,
who made heaven and earth.

PSALM PRAYER

Lord Jesus,
we are truly your disciples,
when reviled and persecuted for your sake.
Be with us in our time of trouble
and free us like birds from a snare.
You live and reign, now and for ever.
~*Amen.*

READING   *1 John 3:14–17*

Sisters and brothers, we know that we have
passed from death to life because we love one
another. Whoever does not love abides in
death. All who hate a brother or sister are murderers, and you know that murderers do not

have eternal life abiding in them. We know love by this, that Christ laid down his life for us— and we ought to lay down our lives for one another. How does God's love abide in anyone who has the world's goods and sees a brother or sister in need and yet refuses to help?

SILENCE

RESPONSE

How good it is to give thanks to you.
~*To sing to your name every evening.*

CANTICLE OF PRAISE OF SAINT FRANCIS OF ASSISI

Holy, holy, holy Lord God Almighty,
who is and who was and who is to come:
Let us praise and glorify him forever.

O Lord our God, you are worthy to receive
praise and glory and honor and blessing:
Let us praise and glorify him forever.

The Lamb of God who was slain is worthy
to receive power and divinity,
and wisdom and strength,
and honor and glory and blessing:
Let us praise and glorify him forever.

Let us bless the Father and the Son with the
Holy Spirit:
Let us praise and glorify him forever.

Bless the Lord, all you works of the Lord:
Let us praise and glorify him forever.

Sing praise to our God, all you his servants
and you who fear God, the small and the great:
Let us praise and glorify him forever.

Let heaven and earth praise him who is glorious:
Let us praise and glorify him forever.

And every creature that is in heaven and on earth
and under the earth and in the sea and those
which are in them:
Let us praise and glorify him forever.

Glory to the Father and to the Son and to the
Holy Spirit:
Let us praise and glorify him forever.

As it was in the beginning, is now, and will be
forever. Amen.
Let us praise and glorify him forever.

INTERCESSIONS

In you, O LORD, I take refuge.
~*Let me never be put to shame.*

In your justice rescue me, free me.
~*Pay heed to me and save me.*

Be a rock where I can take refuge.
~*A mighty stronghold to save me.*

It is you, O Lord, who are my hope.
~*My trust, O Lord, since my youth.*

O God, do not stay far off.
~*My God, make haste to help me!*

LORD'S PRAYER

CLOSING PRAYER

All-powerful, most holy, most high, and
    supreme God:
all good, supreme good, totally good,
you who alone are good;
may we give you all praise, all glory,
all thanks, all honor,
all blessing, and all good things.
So be it. So be it.
~*Amen.*

May the God of all grace who has called us to
eternal glory in Christ + restore, establish and
strengthen us.
~*Amen.*

O Lord, + open my lips.
~*And my mouth shall declare your praise.*

Blest be the precious and life-giving cross
of our Lord Jesus Christ.
~*Now and always and for ever and ever. Amen.*

HYMN

PSALM 22:2–12, 15–21

*They tear holes in my hands and my feet and lay
me in the dust of death.*

My God, my God, why have you forsaken me?
You are far from my plea and the cry of
my distress.
O my God, I call by day and you give me
no reply;
I call by night and I find no peace.

Yet you, O God, are holy,
enthroned on the praises of Israel.
In you our forebears put their trust;
they trusted and you set them free.
When they cried to you, they escaped.
In you they trusted and never in vain.

But I am a worm and no man,
the butt of all, the laughing-stock of the people.
All who see me deride me.
They curl their lips, they toss their heads.
"He trusted in the LORD, let him save him,
and release him if this is his friend."

Yes, it was you who took me from the womb,
entrusted me to my mother's breast.
To you I was committed from my birth,
from my mother's womb you have been
   my God.
Do not leave me alone in my distress;
come close, there is none else to help.

Like water I am poured out,
disjointed are all my bones.
My heart has become like wax,
it is melted within my breast.
Parched as burnt clay is my throat,
my tongue cleaves to my jaws.

Many dogs have surrounded me,
a band of the wicked beset me.
They tear holes in my hands and my feet
and lay me in the dust of death.

I can count every one of my bones.
These people stare at me and gloat;
they divide my clothing among them.
They cast lots for my robe.

O LORD, do not leave me alone,
my strength, make haste to help me!
Rescue my soul from the sword,
my life from the grip of these dogs.

PSALM PRAYER

Good Jesus, friend of all,
I kneel before you hanging on the cross
and recall with sorrow and affection
your five precious wounds,
while I ponder the prophetic words
of King David your ancestor:
"They tear holes in my hands and my feet.
I can count every one of my bones."
Good Jesus, crucified for me,
fix this image of yourself in my heart;
fill me with faith, hope and love.
Make me truly sorry for my sins
and utterly committed to your gospel.
~*Amen.*

READING   *1 Corinthians 1:18, 21–24*

Sisters and brothers, the message about the
cross is foolishness to those who are perishing,
but to us who are being saved it is the power
of God. For since, in the wisdom of God, the
world did not know God through wisdom, God
decided, through the foolishness of our proclamation, to save those who believe. For Jews

demand signs and Greeks desire wisdom, but
we proclaim Christ crucified, a stumbling block
to Jews and foolishness to Gentiles, but to
those who are the called, both Jews and Greeks,
Christ the power of God and the wisdom
of God.

Silence

Response

He carried our sins in his body.
~*To the tree of the cross.*

CANTICLE OF THE SUFFERING SERVANT OF GOD   *Isaiah 53:6-9, 12*

In the cross is victory; in the cross is power.

All we like sheep have gone astray;
we have all turned to our own way,
and the LORD has laid on him the iniquity
   of us all.

He was oppressed, and he was afflicted,
yet he did not open his mouth;
like a lamb that is led to the slaughter,
and like a sheep that before its shearers is silent,
so he did not open his mouth.

By a perversion of justice he was taken away.
Who could have imagined his future?
For he was cut off from the land of the living,
stricken for the transgression of my people.

They made his grave with the wicked
and his tomb with the rich,
although he had done no violence,
and there was no deceit in his mouth.

Therefore I will allot him a portion with
   the great,
and he shall divide the spoil with the strong;
because he poured out himself to death,
and was numbered with the transgressors;
yet he bore the sin of many,
and made intercession for the transgressors.

Glory to God: Creator, Redeemer, and Sanctifier,
now and always and for ever and ever. Amen.

LORD'S PRAYER

CLOSING PRAYER

Lord Jesus Christ,
exposed to the gaze of all on the hill of Calvary,
wash us in your precious blood
and sign us with your mighty cross.
Raise up the dead who sleep in peace,
and save us from the evil one,

O Savior of the world,
living and reigning for ever and ever.
~*Amen.*

May the glorious passion of our Lord Jesus
Christ + bring us to the joys of paradise.
~*Amen.*

FRIDAY EVENING

Jesus Christ + is the light of the world.
~*A light no darkness can extinguish.*

HYMN

PSALM 141:1–9

Father! Into your hands I commend my spirit.

I have called to you, LORD; hasten to help me!
Hear my voice when I cry to you.
Let my prayer arise before you like incense,
the raising of my hands like an evening oblation.

Set, O LORD, a guard over my mouth;
keep watch, O Lord, at the door of my lips!
Do not turn my heart to things that are wrong,
to evil deeds with those who are sinners.

Never allow me to share in their feasting.
If the upright strike or reprove me it is kindness;
but let the oil of the wicked not anoint my head.
Let my prayer be ever against their malice.

Their leaders were thrown down by the side
of the rock;
then they understood that my words were kind.
As a millstone is shattered to pieces on
the ground,
so their bones were strewn at the mouth
of the grave.

To you, LORD God, my eyes were turned;
in you I take refuge; spare my soul!
From the trap they have laid for me keep
me safe;
keep me from the snares of those who do evil.

PSALM PRAYER

Almighty and everlasting God,
may our prayers rise like incense before you,
our hands, like an evening oblation.
As we contemplate your presence
in word and sacrament
and in the lives of our brothers and sisters,
rekindle in us the fire of that love which Jesus
your Son
brought on earth by his passion

and which burns in our hearts by
   the Holy Spirit;
you are one God through all the ages of ages.
~*Amen.*

READING   *1 Corinthians 11:23–26*

Brothers and sisters, I received from the Lord
what I also handed on to you, that the Lord
Jesus on the night when he was betrayed
took a loaf of bread, and when he had given
thanks, he broke it and said, "This is my body
that is for you. Do this in remembrance of
me." In the same way he took the cup also, after
supper, saying, "This cup is the new covenant
in my blood. Do this, as often as you drink it, in
remembrance of me." For as often as you eat
this bread and drink the cup, you proclaim the
Lord's death until he comes.

SILENCE

RESPONSE

Whoever comes to me will never be hungry.
~*And whoever believes in me will never be
thirsty.*

CANTICLE OF OUR EXALTED LORD
Philippians 2:6–11

*Jesus is the Lamb of God who takes away the
sins of the world.*

Though he was in the form of God,
Christ Jesus did not regard equality with God
as something to be exploited,
but emptied himself,
taking the form of a slave,
being born in human likeness.

And being found in human form,
he humbled himself
and became obedient to the point of death—
even death on a cross.

Therefore God highly exalted him
and gave him the name
that is above every name,

so that at the name of Jesus
every knee should bend,
in heaven and on earth and under the earth,
and every tongue should confess
that Jesus Christ is Lord,
to the glory of God the Father.

INTERCESSIONS

Jesus, Savior of the world.
~Come to us in your mercy.

By your cross and precious blood
that set your people free.
~Come to us in your mercy.

You saved your disciples
when they were almost drowning.
~Come to us in your mercy.

In your great mercy loosen us from our sins.
~Come to us in your mercy.

Make yourself known as our Savior
and mighty deliverer.
~Come to us in your mercy.

Draw near according to your promise
from the throne of your glory.
~Come to us in your mercy.

Come again and live among us, Lord Jesus,
and stay with us for ever.
~Come to us in your mercy.

When you come again in power and glory,
make us like you in your glorious kingdom.
~Come to us in your mercy.

LORD'S PRAYER

CLOSING PRAYER

By your holy cross, Lord Jesus,
the church is redeemed, sanctified
and raised on high.

Protect us, O Lord, who take refuge
under the wings of your cross
and bathe us in the precious blood and water
that gushed from your wounded side,
O Savior of the world,
living and reigning for ever and ever.
~*Amen.*

May the glorious passion of our Lord Jesus
Christ **+** bring us to the joys of paradise.
~*Amen.*

SATURDAY MORNING

O Lord, **+** open my lips.
~*And my mouth shall declare your praise.*

Blest be the Lord our God, ruler of the universe.
~*Now and always and for ever and ever.*

HYMN

PSALM 100

They will become one flock and one shepherd.

Cry out with joy to the LORD, all the earth.
Serve the LORD with gladness.
Come before God, singing for joy.

Know that the LORD is God,
Our Maker, to whom we belong.
We are God's people, sheep of the flock.

Enter the gates with thanksgiving,
God's courts with songs of praise.
Give thanks to God and bless his name.

Indeed, how good is the LORD,
whose merciful love is eternal;
whose faithfulness lasts forever.

PSALM PRAYER

Good Shepherd of the flock,
you made us and we belong to you,
our first beginning and our last end.
In union with all your rejoicing saints,
we praise you for your enduring love,
in and through Christ our Lord.
~*Amen.*

READING   *Luke 10:25 – 28*

A lawyer stood up to test Jesus. "Teacher," he
said, "what must I do to inherit eternal life?"
He said to him, "What is written in the law?
What do you read there?" He answered, "You
shall love the Lord your God with all your
heart, and with all your soul, and with all your
strength, and with all your mind; and your

neighbor as yourself." And he said to him, "You have given the right answer; do this, and you will live."

SILENCE

RESPONSE
Delight in the Lord's teaching.
~*And study it night and day.*

CANTICLE OF JUDITH   *Judith 16:13–16*
I sing to my God a fresh, new song.

I will sing to my God a new song:
O Lord, you are great and glorious,
wonderful in strength, invincible.

Let all your creatures serve you,
for you spoke, and they were made.
You sent forth your spirit, and it formed them;
there is none that can resist your voice.

For the mountains shall be shaken
to their foundations with the waters;
before your glance the rocks shall melt like wax.
But to those who fear you
you show mercy.

For every sacrifice as a fragrant offering is a
    small thing,
and the fat of all whole burnt offerings to you is
    a very little thing;
but whoever fears the Lord is great forever.

To the King of the ages, immortal, invisible,
the only wise God,
be honor and glory, through Jesus Christ,
for ever and ever. Amen.

LORD'S PRAYER

CLOSING PRAYER

Almighty God,
unto whom all hearts are open,
all desires known,
and from whom no secrets are hidden:
Cleanse the thoughts of our hearts
by the inspiration of your Holy Spirit,
that we may perfectly love you
and worthily praise your holy name,
through Christ our Lord.
~*Amen.*

May the Word made flesh, full of grace and
truth, + bless us and keep us.
~*Amen.*

Prayer is the key of morning and the bolt
of evening.

~*Mohandas Gandhi, 1869–1948*

FOURTH WEEK

Christ **+** has died, Christ is risen.
~*Christ will come again.*

HYMN

PSALM 125

Lord, you surround your people.

Those who put their trust in the LORD
are like Mount Zion, that cannot be shaken,
that stands for ever.

Jerusalem! The mountains surround her,
so the LORD surrounds his people
both now and for ever.

For the scepter of the wicked shall not rest
over the land of the just
for fear that the hands of the just
should turn to evil.

Do good, LORD, to those who are good,
to the upright of heart;
but the crooked and those who do evil,
drive them away!

On Israel, peace!

PSALM PRAYER

Source of peace and rest,
surround your people
and grant them the peace
that passes all understanding.
Solid and strong in your love,
may we be the church you desire
and serve the needs of humanity,
now and for ever.
~*Amen.*

READING   *Romans 13:8–10*

Brothers and sisters, owe no one anything,
except to love one another; for the one who loves
another has fulfilled the law. The commandments,
"You shall not commit adultery; You
shall not murder; You shall not steal; You shall
not covet"; and any other commandment, are
summed up in this word, "Love your neighbor
as yourself." Love does no wrong to a neighbor; therefore, love is the fulfilling of the law.

SILENCE

RESPONSE

From sunrise to sunset:
~*Praise the name of the Lord.*

CANTICLE OF CHRIST OUR PASSOVER
*1 Corinthians 5:7–8; Romans 6:9–11;
1 Corinthians 15:20–22*

> *God has put all things in subjection under
> Christ's feet.*

Christ our Passover has been sacrificed for us;
therefore let us keep the feast,
Not with the old leaven, the leaven of malice
and evil,
but with the unleavened bread of sincerity and
truth. Alleluia!

Christ being raised from the dead will
never die again;
death no longer has dominion over him.
The death that he died, he died to sin,
once for all;
but the life he lives, he lives to God.
So also consider yourselves dead to sin,
and alive to God in Jesus Christ our Lord.
Alleluia!

Christ has been raised from the dead,
the first fruits of those who have fallen asleep.
For since by a man came death,
by a man has come also the resurrection
   of the dead.
For as in Adam all die,
so also in Christ shall all be made alive. Alleluia!

Glory to the Father, and to the Son,
and to the Holy Spirit:
as it was in the beginning, is now,
and will be for ever. Amen.

APOSTLES' CREED

INTERCESSIONS

Come, Spirit of wisdom, and teach us to value
the highest gifts.
~*Come, Holy Spirit.*

Come, Spirit of understanding, and show us
all things in the light of eternity.
~*Come, Holy Spirit.*

Come, Spirit of counsel, and guide us along the
straight and narrow path to our heavenly home.
~*Come, Holy Spirit.*

Come, Spirit of might, and strengthen us
against every evil interest that would separate
us from you.
~*Come, Holy Spirit.*

Come, Spirit of knowledge, and teach us the shortness of life and the length of eternity.
~*Come, Holy Spirit.*

Come, Spirit of godliness, and stir up our minds and hearts to love and serve the Lord our God all our days.
~*Come, Holy Spirit.*

Come, Spirit of the fear of the Lord, and make us tremble with awe and reverence before your divine majesty.
~*Come, Holy Spirit.*

LORD'S PRAYER

Let us pray as Jesus taught us:
~*Our Father . . .*

CLOSING PRAYER

Heavenly King, Consoler, Spirit of truth, present in all places and filling all things, treasury of blessings and giver of life:
Come and dwell in us.
Cleanse us from every stain of sin
and save our souls,
O gracious Lord.
~*Amen.*

Peace be with the whole community, and love
with faith, from God the Father **+** and the
Lord Jesus Christ.
~Amen.

SUNDAY MORNING

O Lord, **+** open my lips.
~And my mouth shall declare your praise.

This is the day of the Lord's victory! Alleluia!
~Let us rejoice! Alleluia!

HYMN

PSALM 68:2–7, 18–21

*You ascended to the heights, O Christ; you took
captivity captive! Alleluia!*

Let God arise, let the foes be scattered.
Let those who hate God take to flight.
As smoke is blown away so will they
    be blown away;
like wax that melts before the fire,
so the wicked shall perish at the presence
    of God.

But the just shall rejoice at the presence of God,
they shall exult and dance for joy.
O sing to the Lord, make music to God's name;
make a highway for the One who rides
    on the clouds.
Rejoice in the LORD, exult before God.

Father of the orphan, defender of the widow,
such is God in the holy place.
God gives the lonely a home to live in;
and leads the prisoners forth into freedom;
but rebels must dwell in a parched land.

The chariots of God are thousands
    upon thousands.
The Lord has come from Sinai to the holy place.
You have gone up on high; you have taken
    captives,
receiving people in tribute, O God,
even those who rebel, into your dwelling,
    O LORD.

May the Lord be blessed day after day.
God our savior bears our burdens;
this God of ours is a God who saves.

PSALM PRAYER

Lord our God,
in your wisdom and by your power,
you destroyed death's grip on us

by raising your Son from the grave.
You lifted him from the tomb,
gave him the name above all names
and established him in glory.
As we bend our knee before his holy name,
may we worship him by our lives
and witness to him by our love.
We ask this through the same Christ our Lord.
~*Amen.*

READING   *Mark 16:6–7*

The angel said to the women, "Do not be
alarmed; you are looking for Jesus of Nazareth,
who was crucified. He has been raised; he is
not here. Look, there is the place they laid him.
But go, tell his disciples and Peter that he is
going ahead of you to Galilee; there you will see
him, just as he told you."

SILENCE

RESPONSE

Your cross, O Lord, is the tree of life! Alleluia!
~*Bearing fruit for life eternal! Alleluia!*

CANTICLE OF ZACHARY   *Luke 1:68–79*

We are Easter people and alleluia is our song!

Now bless **+** the God of Israel,
Who comes in love and power,
Who raises from the royal house
Deliverance in this hour.

Through holy prophets God has sworn
To free us from alarm,
To save us from the heavy hand
Of all who wish us harm.

Remembering the covenant,
God rescues us from fear,
That we might serve in holiness
And peace from year to year.

And you, my child, shall go before
To preach, to prophesy,
That all may know the tender love,
The grace of God most high.

In tender mercy, God will send
The dayspring from on high,
Our rising Sun, the light of life
For those who sit and sigh.

God comes to guide our way to peace,
That death shall reign no more.
Sing praises to the Holy One!
O worship and adore!

APOSTLES' CREED

LORD'S PRAYER

Let us pray as Jesus taught us:
~*Our Father* . . .

CLOSING PRAYER

God and Father of our Lord Jesus Christ,
by your infinite goodness
we are a chosen people, a royal priesthood,
a consecrated people,
set apart to sing your praises.
Help us to live honorably and unselfishly in
   this world
and so arrive at the glories of the celestial city.
In union with the whole company of heaven,
we shall sing of your majestic deeds,
for ever and ever.
~*Amen.*

Peace be with the whole community, and love
with faith, from God the Father **+** and the
Lord Jesus Christ.
~*Amen.*

Jesus Christ **+** is the light of the world.
~A light no darkness can extinguish.

Christ is risen! Alleluia!
~He is risen indeed! Alleluia!

HYMN

PSALM 86:1–10, 12–13

*Your love for me is great! Alleluia! You have
saved me from the depths of the grave! Alleluia!*

Turn your ear, O LORD, and give answer
for I am poor and needy.
Preserve my life, for I am faithful;
save the servant who trusts in you.

You are my God, have mercy on me, Lord,
for I cry to you all the day long.
Give joy to your servant, O Lord,
for to you I lift up my soul.

O Lord, you are good and forgiving,
full of love to all who call.
Give heed, O LORD, to my prayer
and attend to the sound of my voice.

In the day of distress I will call
and surely you will reply.
Among the gods there is none like you, O Lord,
nor work to compare with yours.

All the nations shall come to adore you
and glorify your name, O Lord,
for you are great and do marvelous deeds,
you who alone are God.

I will praise you, Lord my God, with all
    my heart
and glorify your name, for ever;
for your love to me has been great,
you have saved me from the depths of the grave.

Psalm Prayer

Abba, Father of us all,
you heard your dear Son
when he cried out to you on the cross.
Watch over us, O Lord;
bring us help and comfort.
Stir our desire to revere your name
and to serve our brothers and sisters in Christ.
In Jesus' name.
~Amen.

READING *1 Corinthians 15:50–52*

Brothers and sisters, flesh and blood cannot inherit the kingdom of God, nor does the perishable inherit the imperishable. Listen, I will tell you a mystery! We will not all die, but we will all be changed, in a moment, in the twinkling of an eye, at the last trumpet. For the trumpet will sound, and the dead will be raised imperishable, and we will all be changed.

SILENCE

RESPONSE

Sleeper, awake! Rise from the dead.
~*And Christ will shine on you.*

CANTICLE OF MARY *Luke 1:46–55*

Holy Mother of the risen Christ, you are more worthy of honor than the cherubim and far more glorious than the seraphim!

My soul **+** proclaims the greatness of the Lord.
My spirit sings to God, my saving God,
Who on this day above all others favored me
And raised me up, a light for all to see.

Through me great deeds will God make
 manifest,
And all the earth will come to call me blest.
Unbounded love and mercy sure will I proclaim
For all who know and praise God's holy name.

God's mighty arm, protector of the just,
Will guard the weak and raise them
 from the dust.
But mighty kings will swiftly fall
 from thrones corrupt.
The strong brought low, the lowly lifted up.

Soon will the poor and hungry of the earth
Be richly blest, be given greater worth.
And Israel, as once foretold to Abraham,
Will live in peace throughout the promised land.

All glory be to God, Creator blest,
To Jesus Christ, God's love made manifest,
And to the Holy Spirit, gentle Comforter,
All glory be, both now and evermore. Amen.

INTERCESSIONS

Show us your mercy, O Lord.
~*And grant us your salvation.*

Clothe your ministers with righteousness.
~*Let your people sing with joy.*

Give peace, O Lord, in all the world.
~*For only in you can we live in safety.*

Lord, keep this nation under your care.
~*And guide us in the way of justice and truth.*

Let your way be known upon earth.
~*Your saving health among all nations.*

Let not the needy, O Lord, be forgotten.
~*Nor the hope of the poor be taken away.*

Create in us clean hearts, O God.
~*And sustain us with your Holy Spirit.*

LORD'S PRAYER

CLOSING PRAYER

Only-begotten Son and eternal Word of God,
for our salvation you took flesh
and came to live among us.
You were nailed to the cross,
conquered death by your own death,
and rose again on the third day.
Raise us up with you,
refresh your church,
and make all things new,
O Savior of the world,
living and reigning with the Father and the
    Holy Spirit,
one God, now and for ever.
~*Amen.*

Peace be with the whole community, and love
with faith, from God the Father **+** and the
Lord Jesus Christ.
~Amen.

MONDAY MORNING

O Lord, **+** open my lips.
~And my mouth shall declare your praise.

Glory to God in the highest.
~And peace to those of good will.

HYMN

PSALM 145:1–13

> *You are the Son of God! You are the ruler
> of Israel!*

I will give you glory, O God my king,
I will bless your name for ever.

I will bless you day after day
and praise your name for ever.
You are great, LORD, highly to be praised,
your greatness cannot be measured.

Age to age shall proclaim your works,
shall declare your mighty deeds,
shall speak of your splendor and glory,
tell the tale of your wonderful works.
They will speak of your terrible deeds,
recount your greatness and might.
They will recall your abundant goodness;
age to age shall ring out your justice.

You are kind and full of compassion,
slow to anger, abounding in love.
How good you are, LORD, to all,
compassionate to all your creatures.

All your creatures shall thank you, O LORD,
and your friends shall repeat their blessing.
They shall speak of the glory of your reign
and declare your might, O God,

to make known to all your mighty deeds
and the glorious splendor of your reign.
Yours is an everlasting kingdom;
your rule lasts from age to age.

PSALM PRAYER
Gracious Friend of humanity,
splendid in all your wonderful works,
help us to stand before you

in purity and holiness of life
and reverently serve you as our Creator,
now and for ever.
~*Amen.*

READING   *Romans 5:1–2*

Sisters and brothers, since we are justified
by faith, we have peace with God through our
Lord Jesus Christ, through whom we have
obtained access to this grace in which we stand;
and we boast in our hope of sharing the glory
of God.

SILENCE

RESPONSE

O God, my God, I long for you:
~*From break of day.*

CANTICLE OF REJOICING   *Isaiah 12:2–6*

Let anyone who is thirsty, come to me and drink.

Behold God is my salvation:
I will trust and will not be afraid,
for the Lord God is my strength and my song:
and has become my salvation.

With joy you will draw water
from the wells of salvation:
And in that day all of you will say,

"Give thanks and call upon the name
   of the Lord:
make known among the nations what the Lord
   has done,
proclaim that the name of the Lord is exalted.

"Sing praises for the Lord has triumphed
   gloriously:
let this be known in all the earth.
Shout and sing for joy you people of God:
for great in your midst is the Holy One."

To the King of the ages, immortal, invisible,
the only wise God,
be honor and glory, through Jesus Christ,
for ever and ever. Amen.

LORD'S PRAYER

CLOSING PRAYER

Lord of the universe,
in heaven you established the ordered ranks
of angels and archangels
to celebrate your glory.
As we begin this new day,
may the angels surround and assist us

to serve and glorify your goodness,
for all glory, honor and worship are your due,
Father, Son, and Holy Spirit,
now and always and for ever and ever.
~*Amen.*

May the God of hope fill us with all joy and
peace in believing so that by the power of the
Holy Spirit **+** we may abound in hope.
~*Amen.*

MONDAY EVENING

Light **+** and peace in Jesus Christ our Lord.
~*Thanks be to God.*

HYMN

PSALM 130

*Call him Jesus, for he will save his people from
their sins.*

Out of the depths I cry to you, O LORD,
Lord, hear my voice!
O let your ears be attentive
to the voice of my pleading.

If you, O LORD, should mark our guilt,
Lord, who would survive?
But with you is found forgiveness:
for this we revere you.

My soul is waiting for the LORD.
I count on God's word.
My soul is longing for the Lord
more than those who watch for daybreak.
(Let the watchers count on daybreak
and Israel on the LORD.)

Because with the LORD there is mercy
and fullness of redemption,
Israel indeed God will redeem
from all its iniquity.

PSALM PRAYER
Merciful God,
we are baptized into the death of your dear Son.
May we die to all sin and selfishness
and eagerly await the dawning of our joyful
    resurrection;
by the merits of the same Christ our Lord.
~Amen.

READING   *Romans 6:3 – 4*
Sisters and brothers, do you not know that all
of us who have been baptized into Christ Jesus
were baptized into his death? Therefore we

have been buried with him by baptism into
death, so that, just as Christ was raised from the
dead by the glory of the Father, so we too
might walk in newness of life.

SILENCE

RESPONSE

God's wings will cover you;
~*You will be safe in God's care.*

CANTICLE OF SALVATION
2 Timothy 2:8, 11–13

> *Remember Jesus Christ; we will reign with him.*

Remember Jesus Christ,
raised from the dead,
a descendant of David—
that is my gospel.

If we have died with him,
we will also live with him;
if we endure,
we will also reign with him;

if we deny him,
he will also deny us;
if we are faithless,
he remains faithful—
for he cannot deny himself.

Glory to the Father, and to the Son,
and to the Holy Spirit:
as it was in the beginning, is now,
and will be for ever. Amen.

INTERCESSIONS

Protect your people, Lord:
~*And cause truth and love to reign in your church.*

Bless our cities and farms:
~*And give us the fruits of the earth.*

Grant governments the gifts of wisdom and counsel:
~*And a genuine desire for peace.*

Free prisoners and refugees; defend the oppressed:
~*And put an end to social injustice.*

Forgive our persecutors and oppressors:
~*And heal religious and political strife.*

Grant eternal rest to our dear departed:
~*Who have fallen asleep in Christ.*

LORD'S PRAYER

CLOSING PRAYER

Heavenly Father,
let those for whom we pray,
whether still detained in this life
or already living in the next,
obtain from your loving-kindness
the full forgiveness of their sins
and all that is helpful to their salvation,
through Jesus Christ our Lord.
~Amen.

May the God of hope fill us with all joy and
peace in believing so that by the power of the
Holy Spirit **+** we may abound in hope.
~Amen.

TUESDAY MORNING

O Lord, **+** open my lips.
~And my mouth shall declare your praise.

Blest be the Lord our God, the ruler of
the universe.
~Now and always and for ever and ever.

HYMN

PSALM 146

Your God reigns for ever, from age to age.

My soul, give praise to the LORD;
I will praise the LORD all my days,
make music to my God while I live.

Put no trust in the powerful,
mere mortals in whom there is no help.
Take their breath, they return to clay
and their plans that day come to nothing.

They are happy who are helped by Jacob's God,
whose hope is in the LORD their God,
who alone made heaven and earth,
the seas and all they contain.

It is the Lord who keeps faith for ever,
who is just to those who are oppressed.
It is God who gives bread to the hungry,
the LORD, who sets prisoners free,

the LORD who gives sight to the blind,
who raises up those who are bowed down,
the LORD, who protects the stranger
and upholds the widow and orphan.

It is the LORD who loves the just
but thwarts the path of the wicked.
The LORD will reign for ever,
Zion's God from age to age.

PSALM PRAYER

God of might and majesty,
Creator of heaven and earth,
you keep faith with us for ever.
Rescue the troubled and afflicted,
set us free from all our sins,
and preserve us in your truth,
through Christ our Lord.
~*Amen.*

READING   *Romans 6:5–8*

Brothers and sisters, if we have been united
with Christ in a death like his, we will certainly
be united with him in a resurrection like his. We
know that our old self was crucified with him
so that the body of sin might be destroyed, and
we might no longer be enslaved to sin. For
whoever has died is freed from sin. But if we
have died with Christ, we believe that we will
also live with him.

SILENCE

RESPONSE

Fill us each morning with your constant love:
~*So that we may sing and be glad all our life.*

CANTICLE OF GOD'S SERVANT
Isaiah 61:1–3, 10–11

*God has clothed me with the garments
of salvation.*

The spirit of the Lord GOD is upon me,
because the LORD has anointed me;
the LORD has sent me to bring good news
   to the oppressed,
to bind up the brokenhearted,
to proclaim liberty to the captives,
and release to the prisoners;

to proclaim the year of the LORD's favor,
and the day of vengeance of our God;
to comfort all who mourn;
to provide for those who mourn in Zion—
to give them a garland instead of ashes,
the oil of gladness instead of mourning,
the mantle of praise instead of a faint spirit.
They will be called oaks of righteousness,
the planting of the LORD, to display the glory
   of God.

I will greatly rejoice in the LORD,
my whole being shall exult in my God;
for God has clothed me with the garments
    of salvation,
and has covered me with the robe
    of righteousness,
as a bridegroom decks himself with a garland,
and as a bride adorns herself with her jewels.

For as the earth brings forth its shoots,
and as a garden causes what is sown in it
    to spring up,
so the Lord GOD will cause righteousness
    and praise
to spring up before all the nations.

Glory to God: Creator, Redeemer, and Sanctifier,
now and always and for ever and ever. Amen.

LORD'S PRAYER

CLOSING PRAYER

Gracious God and Father,
accept our morning worship of praise
    and prayer.
Give us unshakable faith, firm hope
    and sincere love;
bless our comings and our goings,

our deeds and our desires,
our work and our prayer.
In Jesus' name.
~*Amen.*

May the God of peace sanctify us, and
may our spirit, soul and body **+** be kept
sound and blameless at the coming of
our Lord Jesus Christ.
~*Amen.*

TUESDAY EVENING

The Word **+** was the source of life.
~*And this life brought light to all.*

HYMN

PSALM 134

Jesus spent the whole night praying to God.

O come, bless the LORD,
all you who serve the LORD,
who stand in the house of the LORD,
in the courts of the house of our God.

Lift up your hands to the holy place
and bless the LORD through the night.

May the LORD bless you from Zion,
God who made heaven and earth.

PSALM PRAYER

Almighty God,
clothe us in the mantle of praise
that we may always rejoice
in proclaiming your glory
and in receiving your blessings,
through Christ our Lord.
~Amen.

READING   *Romans 8:11*

Sisters and brothers, if the Spirit of the one who
raised Jesus from the dead dwells in you, the
one who raised Christ from the dead will give
life to your mortal bodies also through this
Spirit dwelling in you.

SILENCE

RESPONSE

You created the moon to mark the months.
~The sun knows the time to set.

CANTICLE OF LIFE IN THE SPIRIT
Romans 8:2, 14–17a, 18–19

> *The Spirit helps us in our weakness.*

The law of the Spirit of life in Christ Jesus
has set you free from the law of sin and death.

For all who are led by the Spirit of God
are children of God.
For you did not receive a spirit of slavery
to fall back into fear,
but you have received a spirit of adoption.

When we cry, "Abba! dear Father!"
it is that very Spirit bearing witness
    with our spirit
that we are children of God,
and if children, then heirs,
heirs of God and joint heirs with Christ.

I consider that the sufferings of this present time
are not worth comparing with the glory
about to be revealed to us.
For the creation waits with eager longing
for the revealing of the children of God.

Glory to the Father, and to the Son,
and to the Holy Spirit:
as it was in the beginning, is now,
and will be for ever. Amen.

INTERCESSIONS

Lord Jesus Christ, faithful witness and firstborn
from the dead:
~*Be our life and our resurrection.*

High priest of the new and eternal covenant:
~*Intercede for your holy church.*

You who loved us and washed away our sins in
your blood:
~*Make us royal priests to serve our God.*

Living bread, manna from heaven:
~*Be our life-giving food.*

Lamb of God, you take away the sins of the
world:
~*Grant us your peace.*

LORD'S PRAYER

CLOSING PRAYER

Look down, O Lord,
from your heavenly throne.
Illuminate the darkness of the coming night
with your celestial brightness,
and from the children of light
banish the deeds of darkness,
through Jesus Christ our Lord.
~*Amen.*

May the God of peace sanctify us, and
may our spirit, soul and body **+** be kept
sound and blameless at the coming of
our Lord Jesus Christ.
~*Amen.*

WEDNESDAY MORNING

O Lord, **+** open my lips.
~*And my mouth shall declare your praise.*

Blest be the holy and undivided Trinity.
~*Now and for ever.*

HYMN

PSALM 148

God is the praise of all the saints!

Praise the LORD from the heavens,
praise God in the heights.
Praise God, all you angels,
praise him, all you hosts.

Praise God, sun and moon,
praise him, shining stars.
Praise God, highest heavens
and the waters above the heavens.

Let them praise the name of the LORD.
The Lord commanded: they were made.
God fixed them forever,
gave a law which shall not pass away.

Praise the LORD from the earth,
sea creatures and all oceans,
fire and hail, snow and mist,
stormy winds that obey God's word;

all mountains and hills,
all fruit trees and cedars,
beasts, wild and tame,
reptiles and birds on the wing;

all earth's nations and peoples,
earth's leaders and rulers;
young men and maidens,
the old together with children.

Let them praise the name of the LORD
who alone is exalted.
The splendor of God's name
reaches beyond heaven and earth.

God exalts the strength of the people,
is the praise of all the saints,
of the sons and daughters of Israel,
of the people to whom he comes close.

PSALM PRAYER

With the heavenly hosts
of glowing angels and glittering stars,
may all that takes its origin from you
praise and glorify your magnificent name,
Father, Son, and Holy Spirit,
now and for ever.
~*Amen.*

READING   *Romans 8:26–27*

Brothers and sisters, the Spirit helps us in
our weakness; for we do not know how to pray
as we ought, but that very Spirit intercedes
with sighs too deep for words. And God, who
searches the heart, knows what is the mind
of the Spirit, because the Spirit intercedes for
the saints according to the will of God.

SILENCE

RESPONSE

Awake, my harp and lyre.
~*I will wake up the sun.*

CANTICLE OF JEREMIAH   *Jeremiah 7:2–7*

*Go and learn what this means: "I desire mercy,
not sacrifice."*

Hear the word of the LORD,
all you people of Judah,
you that enter these gates
to worship the LORD.

Thus says the LORD of hosts,
the God of Israel:
Amend your ways and your doings,
and let me dwell with you in this place.
Do not trust in these deceptive words:
"This is the temple of the LORD,
the temple of the LORD,
the temple of the LORD."

If you truly amend your ways and your doings,
if you truly act justly one with another,
if you do not oppress the alien,
the orphan, and the widow,
or shed innocent blood in this place,
and if you do not go after other gods to your
    own hurt,
then I will dwell with you in this place,
in the land that I gave of old to your ancestors
forever and ever.

To the King of the ages, immortal, invisible,
the only wise God,
be honor and glory, through Jesus Christ,
for egver and ever. Amen.

LORD'S PRAYER

CLOSING PRAYER

Compassionate God,
cleanse our hearts of all faults,
fill our minds with divine wisdom,
and open our lips to sing your praise
every morning of our lives.
We ask this through Christ our Lord.
~Amen.

May the God of hope fill us with all joy and
peace in believing so that by the power of the
Holy Spirit **+** we may abound in hope.
~Amen.

WEDNESDAY EVENING

Light **+** and peace in Jesus Christ our Lord.
~Thanks be to God.

HYMN

PSALM 138

Lord, your love lasts for ever.

I thank you, Lord, with all my heart,
you have heard the words of my mouth.
In the presence of the angels I will bless you.
I will adore before your holy temple.

I thank you for your faithfulness and love
which excel all we ever knew of you.
On the day I called, you answered;
you increased the strength of my soul.

All the rulers on earth shall thank you
when they hear the words of your mouth.
They shall sing of the LORD's ways:
"How great is the glory of the LORD!"

The LORD is high yet looks on the lowly
and the haughty God knows from afar.
Though I walk in the midst of affliction
you give me life and frustrate my foes.

You stretch out your hand and save me,
your hand will do all things for me.
Your love, O LORD, is eternal,
discard not the work of your hands.

PSALM PRAYER

Great is your glory, Lord,
and you display your loving-kindness
to all who need it.
Take up our cause
and reach out your right hand
to shelter and save us,
for your love lasts for ever.
~*Amen.*

READING   *Romans 8:31–34*

Sisters and brothers, if God is for us, who
is against us? The very Son of God was
not withheld, but was given up for all of us;
will God not along with the Son also give
us everything else? Who will bring any charge
against God's elect? It is God who justifies.
Who is to condemn? It is Christ Jesus, who died,
yes, who was raised, who is at the right hand of
God, who indeed intercedes for us.

SILENCE

RESPONSE

A light shines in the darkness.
~*For those who are merciful.*

CANTICLE OF PRAISE AND THANKSGIVING

Come, let us worship the true God, One in Three and Three in One! Alleluia!

Holy and blessed Trinity,
Father, Son, and Holy Spirit,
your splendid and glorious name
is worthy of praise from every mouth,
of confession from every heart,
of worship from every human creature,
for you created the world in your grace
and restored it by your compassion
through the victorious cross of your
    beloved Son,
our dear Lord and Savior Jesus Christ.

Before your majestic face, O God,
a myriad of angels and saints bow down in
    adoration,
singing, praising and glorifying you without
    ceasing:

Holy is God, holy and strong, holy and living
    for ever,
heaven and earth are full of your glory.
Blessed are you, Lord, in the highest heavens,
reigning supreme over all creation!
Hosanna in the highest!

INTERCESSIONS

Lord Jesus Christ, daystar from on high,
revelation to the nations.
~Shine in our darkness.

Lord Jesus Christ, light up the world
with the beam of your saving word.
~Shine in our darkness.

Lord Jesus Christ, renew us in the image
and likeness of God.
~Shine in our darkness.

Lord Jesus Christ, lead us to praise you
in thought, word and deed.
~Shine in our darkness.

Lord Jesus Christ, keep us safe
from all sin and danger.
~Shine in our darkness.

LORD'S PRAYER

CLOSING PRAYER

Hear our prayers, O Lord,
and protect us both by night and by day.
Whatever the changes and chances of this
  mortal life,
may we always find strength in your
  unchanging love,
through Jesus Christ our Lord.
~Amen.

May the Lord **+** direct our hearts in the love of
God and the patience of Christ.
~Amen.

THURSDAY MORNING

O Lord, **+** open my lips.
~And my mouth shall declare your praise.

Blest be our God at all times.
~Now and always and for ever and ever.

HYMN

PSALM 149:1–6

Sing praise in the assembly of the faithful.

Sing a new song to the LORD,
Sing praise in the assembly of the faithful.
Let Israel rejoice in its Maker,
let Zion's people exult in their king.
Let them praise God's name with dancing
and make music with timbrel and harp.

For the LORD takes delight in his people,
and crowns the poor with salvation.
Let the faithful rejoice in their glory,
shout for joy and take their rest.
Let the praise of God be on their lips
and a two-edged sword in their hand.

PSALM PRAYER

Christ our Lord,
you are both our way to heaven
and our heavenly home itself.
As you are our Savior here and now,
may we sing for joy in your presence
through all eternity.
~Amen.

READING   *Romans 8:35–39*

Sisters and brothers, who will separate us from
the love of Christ? Will hardship, or distress,
or persecution, or famine, or nakedness, or peril,
or sword? No, in all these things we are more
than conquerors through him who loved us. For
I am convinced that neither death, nor life, nor
angels, nor rulers, nor things present, nor things
to come, nor powers, nor height, nor depth,
nor anything else in all creation, will be able to
separate us from the love of God in Christ Jesus
our Lord.

SILENCE

RESPONSE
More than sentries for dawn:
~*I wait for the Lord.*

CANTICLE OF EZEKIEL *Ezekiel 36:24–28*
You shall be my people and I will be your God.

I will take you from the nations,
and gather you from all the countries,
and bring you into your own land.

I will sprinkle clean water upon you,
and you shall be clean
from all your uncleannesses,
and from all your idols I will cleanse you.

A new heart I will give you,
and a new spirit I will put within you;
and I will remove from your body
the heart of stone
and give you a heart of flesh.

I will put my spirit within you,
and make you follow my statutes
and be careful to observe my ordinances.

Then you shall live in the land
that I gave to your ancestors;
and you shall be my people,
and I will be your God.

LORD'S PRAYER

CLOSING PRAYER

Heavenly King, Consoler, Spirit of truth,
present in all places and filling all things,
treasury of blessings and giver of life:
Come and dwell in us.
Cleanse us from every stain of sin,
and save our souls,
O gracious Lord.
~Amen.

May the God of all grace who has called us to
eternal glory in Christ **+** restore, establish and
strengthen us.
~Amen.

THURSDAY EVENING

I am **+** the light of the world.
~Whoever follows me will walk in beauty.

HYMN

PSALM 139:1–14

Even the hairs of your head are all counted.

O LORD, you search me and you know me,
you know my resting and my rising,
you discern my purpose from afar.
You mark when I walk or lie down,
all my ways lie open to you.

Before ever a word is on my tongue
you know it, O LORD, through and through.
Behind and before you besiege me,
your hand ever laid upon me.
Too wonderful for me, this knowledge,
too high, beyond my reach.

O where can I go from your spirit,
or where can I flee from your face?
If I climb the heavens, you are there.
If I lie in the grave, you are there.

If I take the wings of the dawn
and dwell at the sea's furthest end,
even there your hand would lead me,
your right hand would hold me fast.

If I say: "Let the darkness hide me
and the light around me be night,"
even darkness is not dark for you
and the night is as clear as the day.

For it was you who created my being,
knit me together in my mother's womb.
I thank you for the wonder of my being,
for the wonders of all your creation.

PSALM PRAYER

Lord Jesus,
in the dark desolation of your passion,
you trusted in your God and Father.
You are always present in our hearts,
and by your protecting care
make even darkness as bright as day.
You live and reign now and for ever.
~*Amen.*

READING *Romans 12:1–2*

I appeal to you, brothers and sisters, by the
mercies of God, to present your bodies as
a living sacrifice, holy and acceptable to God,
which is your spiritual worship. Do not be
conformed to this world, but be transformed by
the renewing of your minds, so that you may
discern what is the will of God—what is good
and acceptable and perfect.

SILENCE

RESPONSE

Light shines on the righteous.
~*And gladness on the good.*

CANTICLE OF LIVING HOPE
1 Peter 1:3–7

> *Our faith is more precious than gold.*

Blessed be the God and Father of our Lord
    Jesus Christ:
by whose great mercy we have been born anew,
born to a living hope:
by the resurrection of Jesus Christ from
    the dead;
born to an inheritance
which will never perish or wither away:
one that is kept in heaven for us.

By God's power we are guarded through faith:
for a salvation ready to be revealed at the end
    of time.
We rejoice in this, though now we suffer
    various trials:
so that the genuineness of our faith,
more precious than gold that is tested by fire,
may result in praise and glory and honor
at the revelation of Jesus Christ.

Glory to the Father, and to the Son,
and to the Holy Spirit:
as it was in the beginning, is now,
and will be for ever. Amen.

INTERCESSIONS

God of justice and peace:
~*Free us from the chains of our sins.*

Forgive the sins of those who confess to you:
~*And grant us pardon and peace.*

Bless all ministers of religion:
~*May they desire only what is pleasing to you.*

Guide all civil authorities:
~*Turn their thoughts toward justice and peace.*

Kindle our hearts with the fire of your Spirit:
~*May we serve you with an undivided heart.*

Bless our every prayer and work:
~*Be its beginning and its end.*

Save us in our dying hour:
~*That we may bless you for ever and ever.*

Give a place of refreshment, light and peace:
~*To those who have fallen asleep in Christ.*

LORD'S PRAYER

CLOSING PRAYER

Lord God,
stretch out the right hand of your majesty
over your catholic and apostolic church
spread out across the world.
Preserve it from all harm,
and by your mercy make us worthy
to serve you in purity of heart
and devotion of life,
through Jesus Christ our Lord.
~*Amen.*

May the God of all grace who has called us to
eternal glory in Christ **+** restore, establish and
strengthen us.
~*Amen.*

FRIDAY MORNING

O Lord, **+** open my lips.
~*And my mouth shall declare your praise.*

Come, let us worship Christ our Lord.
~*He was lifted up on the cross for our salvation.*

HYMN

PSALM 28:1-3, 6-9

The good shepherd is willing to die for the sheep.

To you, O LORD, I call,
my rock, hear me.
If you do not heed I shall become
like those in the grave.

Hear the voice of my pleading
as I call for help,
as I lift up my hands in prayer
to your holy place.

Do not drag me away with the wicked,
with the evildoers
who speak words of peace to their neighbors
but with evil in their hearts.

Praise to you, LORD, you have heard
my cry, my appeal.
You, LORD, are my strength and my shield;
in you my heart trusts.
I was helped, my heart rejoices
and I praise you with my song.

LORD, you are the strength of your people,
a fortress where your anointed finds refuge.
Save your people; bless Israel your heritage.
Be their shepherd and carry them for ever.

Psalm Prayer

By your precious cross, O Lord,
you have overthrown
the enemy of humanity.
Grant full pardon and bring fresh salvation
to those numbered among your loyal people
and raise up your servants
who have fallen asleep in death,
O Savior of the world,
living and reigning for ever and ever.
~*Amen.*

READING *Galatians 2:19b–20*

Brothers and sisters, I have been crucified with
Christ; and it is no longer I who live, but it is
Christ who lives in me. And the life I now live
in the flesh I live by faith in the Son of God,
who loved me and gave himself for me.

Silence

Response

By the standard of the cross, O Lord,
~*Deliver us from all sin and danger.*

CANTICLE OF REPENTANCE
Isaiah 55:6–11

Repent and believe in the Good News of God.

Seek the Lord who is still to be found:
call upon God who is yet at hand.
Return to the Lord, who will have compassion:
to our God, who will abundantly pardon.

"For my thoughts are not your thoughts:
nor are your ways my ways," says the Lord.
"For as the heavens are higher than the earth:
so are my ways higher than your ways
and my thoughts than your thoughts.

"For as the rain and snow come down from
     heaven:
and return not again but water the earth,
causing the earth to bring forth and sprout:
giving seed to the sower and bread
     to the hungry;

"so shall my word be that goes forth from
     my mouth:
it shall not return to me empty,
but it shall accomplish that which I desire:
and achieve the purpose for which I sent it."

Glory to God: Creator, Redeemer, and Sanctifier,
now and always and for ever and ever. Amen.

LORD'S PRAYER

CLOSING PRAYER

Lord Jesus Christ, Son of the living God,
set your passion, your cross and your death
between your judgment and our souls,
now and in the hour of our death.
In your goodness,
grant mercy and grace to the living
and forgiveness and rest to the dead.
To the church and to the nations
grant peace and concord,
and to us sinners, life and glory without end.
~Amen.

May the glorious passion of our Lord Jesus
Christ **+** bring us to the joys of paradise.
~Amen.

FRIDAY EVENING

Jesus Christ **+** is the light of the world.
~A light no darkness can extinguish.

HYMN

PSALM 142

*Listen to my cry for help, for I am sunk
in despair.*

With all my voice I cry to you, LORD,
with all my voice I entreat you, LORD.
I pour out my trouble before you;
I tell you all my distress
while my spirit faints within me.
But you, O Lord, know my path.

On the way where I shall walk
they have hidden a snare to entrap me.
Look on my right and see:
there is no one who takes my part.
I have no means of escape,
not one who cares for my soul.

I cry to you, O LORD.
I have said: "You are my refuge,
all I have in the land of the living."
Listen, then, to my cry
for I am in the depths of distress.

Rescue me from those who pursue me
for they are stronger than I.
Bring my soul out of this prison
and then I shall praise your name.
Around me the just will assemble
because of your goodness to me.

PSALM PRAYER

By the power of your cross, O Lord,
set us free from our sins,
save us in the time of trial
and raise us up on the great and final day.
You live and reign, now and for ever.
~*Amen.*

READING   *Mark 10:42–45*

Jesus called his disciples together and said to
them, "You know that among the Gentiles
those whom they recognize as their rulers lord
it over them, and their great ones are tyrants
over them. But it is not so among you; for whoever wishes to become great among you must
be your servant, and whoever wishes to be first
among you must be the slave of all. For the
Son of Man came not to be served but to serve,
and to give his life a ransom for many."

SILENCE

RESPONSE

Blessed be the cross of our Lord Jesus Christ.
~*For in him is our salvation, life and resurrection.*

CANTICLE OF GOD'S PEOPLE
1 Peter 2:4–5, 9–10

*The stone the builders rejected has become
the cornerstone.*

Come to the Lord, a living stone,
though rejected by mortals
yet chosen and precious in God's sight,
and like living stones,
let yourselves be built into a spiritual house,
to be a holy priesthood, to offer spiritual
    sacrifices
acceptable to God through Jesus Christ.

You are a chosen race, a royal priesthood,
a holy nation, God's own people,
in order that you may proclaim the mighty acts
of him who called you out of darkness
into his marvelous light.

Once you were not a people,
but now you are God's people;
once you had not received mercy,
but now you have received mercy.

Glory to the Father, and to the Son,
and to the Holy Spirit:
as it was in the beginning, is now,
and will be for ever. Amen.

INTERCESSIONS

We adore you, Lord Jesus Christ, ascending
your cross of pain.
*~May this cross deliver us from the destroying
angel.*

We adore your wounded body hanging on
the cross.
~May your precious wounds be our healing.

We adore you dead and buried in the tomb.
~May your death be our life.

We adore you descending among the dead to
deliver them.
*~May we never hear the dreaded sentence
of doom.*

We adore you rising victoriously from the dead.
~Free us from the weight of our sins.

We adore you ascending to the Father.
~Lift us to eternal glory with all your saints.

We adore you coming in glory to judge the
living and the dead.
~Be not our judge but our Savior.

LORD'S PRAYER

CLOSING PRAYER

Lord Jesus Christ,
suffering servant of God,
you were unjustly condemned to death,
mocked, scourged and crowned with thorns,
pierced by nails and scorned.
By your holy and glorious wounds,
guard and keep us from all evil
and bring us to the victory you have won for us.
You live and reign now and for ever.
~*Amen.*

May the glorious passion of our Lord Jesus
Christ + bring us to the joys of paradise.
~*Amen.*

SATURDAY MORNING

O Lord, + open my lips.
~*And my mouth shall declare your praise.*

Blest be the Lord our God, ruler of the universe.
~*Now and always, and for ever and ever.*

HYMN

PSALM 150

You are my praise, O God, in the great assembly.

Praise God in his holy place,
Sing praise in the mighty heavens.
Sing praise for God's powerful deeds,
praise God's surpassing greatness.

Sing praise with sound of trumpet,
Sing praise with lute and harp.
Sing praise with timbrel and dance.
Sing praise with strings and pipes.

Sing praise with resounding cymbals,
Sing praise with clashing of cymbals.
Let everything that lives and that breathes
give praise to the LORD. Alleluia!

PSALM PRAYER

Living and eternal God,
may a harmonious chorus of human praise
blend with the canticles of rejoicing saints
as we devote ourselves to your honor and glory,
Father, Son, and Holy Spirit,
now and for ever.
~Amen.

READING *Romans 12:9–13*

Let love be genuine, sisters and brothers; hate
what is evil, hold fast to what is good; love
one another with mutual affection; outdo one
another in showing honor. Do not lag in zeal,
be ardent in spirit, serve the Lord. Rejoice
in hope, be patient in suffering, persevere in
prayer. Contribute to the needs of the saints;
extend hospitality to strangers.

SILENCE

RESPONSE

Remind me each morning of your constant love:
~*For I put my trust in you.*

CANTICLE OF JEREMIAH
Jeremiah 17:7–8

God alone, my rock, my safety, my refuge!

Blessed are those who trust in the LORD,
whose trust is the LORD.
They shall be like a tree planted by water,
sending out its roots by the stream.

It shall not fear when heat comes,
and its leaves shall stay green;
in the year of drought it is not anxious,
and it does not cease to bear fruit.

Glory to you, Source of all being,
Eternal Word, and Holy Spirit:
as it was in the beginning, is now,
and will be forever. Amen.

LORD'S PRAYER

CLOSING PRAYER

Lord of the dawning day,
be the light of our lives today and every day.
May we serve you with a clean conscience
and give you heartfelt praise
in union with the great Mother of God
and the whole company of heaven.
We ask this through Christ our Lord.
~*Amen.*

May the Word made flesh, full of grace and
truth, **+** bless us and keep us.
~*Amen.*

❈

**By night I will sing to the Lord,
praise the God of my life.**

~Psalm 42:9

❈

NIGHT PRAYER

Night Prayer (Compline) was originally recited in the dormitories of monasteries just before going to bed. It is suitable for single people, couples, families or church groups who wish to round out a full day of work and play.

This order for Night Prayer follows the format of morning and evening prayer. Three psalms and three readings have been provided. Choose one of each, concluding the psalm selected with the doxology.

Our help **+** is in the name of the Lord.
~*The maker of heaven and earth.*

Even darkness is not dark for you, O Lord.
~*And night is clear as day.*

PSALM 31:2-6

In you, O LORD, I take refuge.
Let me never be put to shame.
In your justice, set me free,
hear me and speedily rescue me.

Be a rock of refuge for me,
a mighty stronghold to save me,
for you are my rock, my stronghold.
For your name's sake, lead me and guide me.

Release me from the snares they have hidden
for you are my refuge, Lord.
Into your hands I commend my spirit.
It is you who will redeem me, LORD.

PSALM 131

O LORD, my heart is not proud
nor haughty my eyes.
I have not gone after things too great
nor marvels beyond me.

Truly I have set my soul
in silence and peace.
A weaned child on its mother's breast,
even so is my soul.

O Israel, hope in the LORD
both now and for ever.

PSALM 133

How good and how pleasant it is,
when people live in unity!

It is like precious oil upon the head,
running down upon the beard,
running down upon Aaron's beard,
upon the collar of his robes.

It is like the dew of Hermon which falls
on the heights of Zion.
For there the LORD gives blessing,
life for ever.

DOXOLOGY

To the Ruler of the ages, immortal, invisible,
the only wise God,
Be honor and glory, through Jesus Christ,
for ever and ever. Amen.

READING   *Matthew 11:28–30*

Come to me, all you that are weary and are
carrying heavy burdens, and I will give you rest.
Take my yoke upon you, and learn from me;
for I am gentle and humble in heart, and you
will find rest for your souls. For my yoke is
easy, and my burden is light.

READING   *1 Peter 5:6–9*

Humble yourselves under the mighty hand
of God, so that he may exalt you in due time.
Cast all your anxiety on him, because he
cares for you. Discipline yourselves, keep alert.
Like a roaring lion your adversary the devil
prowls around, looking for someone to devour.
Resist him, steadfast in your faith, for you know
that your brothers and sisters in all the world
are undergoing the same kind of suffering.

READING   *Jeremiah 14:9b*

You, O LORD, are in the midst of us, and we are
called by your name; do not forsake us!

SILENCE

RESPONSE

Into your hands, O Lord, I commend my spirit.
~*You who will redeem me, Lord, God of truth.*

CANTICLE OF SIMEON   *Luke 2:29–32*

Jesus Christ is the light of the world, a light no darkness can conceal.

Now, Lord, + you let your servant go in peace:
your word has been fulfilled.
My own eyes have seen the salvation
which you have prepared in the sight
  of every people:
a light to reveal you to the nations
and the glory of your people Israel.

Glory to the Father, and to the Son,
and to the Holy Spirit:
as it was in the beginning, is now,
and will be for ever. Amen.

INTERCESSIONS

LORD'S PRAYER

CLOSING PRAYER

Guard us, O Lord, while we are awake
and keep us while we sleep,
that waking, we may watch with Christ,
and sleeping, we may rest in peace.
In Jesus' name.
~*Amen.*

MARIAN ANTHEMS

FOR ORDINARY TIME

Hail, holy Queen, Mother of mercy,
hail, our life, our sweetness, and our hope.
To you we cry, the children of Eve;
to you we send up our sighs,
mourning and weeping in this land of exile.
Turn, then, most gracious advocate,
your eyes of mercy toward us;
lead us home at last
and show us the blessed fruit of your womb,
   Jesus:
O clement, O loving, O sweet Virgin Mary.

Pray for us, holy Mother of God,
~*That we may become worthy of the promises
of Christ.*

Almighty and everlasting God,
by the cooperation of the Holy Spirit,
you prepared the humble Virgin Mary
to be a fit dwelling for your beloved Son.
May we who rejoice in her memory
be freed by her loving prayers
both from present ills and from eternal death.
We ask this in Jesus' name.
~*Amen.*

Through the Virgin Mother blest
may the Lord + grant us our rest.
~*Amen.*

FOR ADVENT AND CHRISTMAS SEASON

Mother of Christ, our hope, our patroness,
star of the sea, our beacon in distress.
Guide to the shores of everlasting day
God's holy people on their pilgrim way.

Virgin, in you God made his dwelling-place;
Mother of all the living, full of grace,
blessed are you: God's word you did believe;
"Yes" on your lips undid the "No" of Eve.

Daughter of God, who bore his holy One,
dearest of all to Christ, your loving Son,
show us his face, O Mother, as on earth,
loving us all, you gave our Savior birth.

The Word was made flesh.
~*And lived among us.*

Abba, dear Father,
by the fruitful virginity of the Virgin Mary
you brought life and salvation
to the whole human race.
Grant that we may experience
the power of her intercession
through whom we received the author of life,

our Lord Jesus Christ,
in whose name we pray.
~*Amen.*

May the Virgin Mary mild
+ bless us with her holy Child.
~*Amen.*

FOR LENT

We turn to you for protection,
holy Mother of God.
Listen to our prayers
and help us in our needs.
Save us from every danger,
glorious and blessed Virgin.

May we praise you, O holy Virgin.
~*Give us strength in our hour of need.*

Merciful God and Father,
may we who honor the memory
of the great Mother of God, Mary most holy,
rise from our sins by the help of her prayers.
In the name of Jesus.
~*Amen.*

May Christ, Son of God and Son of Mary,
+ bless us and keep us.
~*Amen.*

For Easter Season

Rejoice, O Queen of heaven, alleluia!
For the Son you bore, alleluia!
Has arisen as he promised, alleluia!
Pray for us to God the Father, alleluia!

Rejoice and be glad, alleluia!
~For the Lord has truly risen, alleluia!

Holy and living God,
joy came into the world
when you lifted your dear Son
from among the dead.
By the prayers of Mary his mother
and of all the myrrh-bearing women,
bring us to the happiness of everlasting life,
through the same Christ our Lord.
~Amen.

By the power of Christ's resurrection
and the prayers of the whole company of
heaven, may God **+** grant us safety and peace.
~Amen.

You move us to delight in praising you
for you have made us for yourself, and
our hearts are restless till they find rest in you.

~Saint Augustine of Hippo, 354–430

APPENDIX

BIBLICAL READINGS THROUGHOUT THE LITURGICAL YEAR

INTRODUCTION

The following Bible readings may take the place of the shorter lessons printed in the four-week cycle. No set length is suggested, but "less is more" because scripture is to be pondered, meditated and digested—not merely read. Modern Bibles usually supply divisions and headings to the text that help the reader select passages of suitable length for daily reading.

Many Bibles also have introductions to each book. These can be helpful when beginning any book that is unfamiliar. Serious students of scripture also need to consult standard introductions and commentaries on the Bible, as well as Bible dictionaries and atlases. Studying scripture in this way prepares us to hear the scripture readings more fruitfully in the liturgy. Our approach to scripture during study is different from our approach during prayer. Hearing scripture in the context of morning and evening prayer stirs up our affections so that we can reach out to the God of love who is revealed in the sacred pages. Study is useful; prayer is necessary.

ADVENT

For about four weeks before Christmas we reflect on scripture that helps us watch and pray for the coming of the Lord.

During the first three weeks choose verses from the prophet Isaiah, the Old Testament "evangelist," who supplies the most appropriate readings for this season of longing and waiting: chapters 1–14, 24–39, 40–55, 60–66.

On the eight days before Christmas, read these passages: December 17: *Isaiah 7:1–17;* December 18: *Isaiah 9:1–7;* December 19: *Isaiah 11:1–9;* December 20: *Isaiah 12:1–6;* December 21: *Isaiah 25:6–12;* December 22: *Isaiah 35:1–10;* December 23: *Isaiah 40:1–11;* December 24: *Isaiah 42:1–9.*

CHRISTMAS SEASON

Although many keep the season from December 25 to the Baptism of the Lord, the scripture readings for the Presentation of the Lord on February 2 seem to close the infancy narratives, so we might continue in the Christmas spirit until then.

Use selections from the first two chapters of the gospels of Matthew and Luke for the Christmas to Epiphany period. Read chapters 60–66 of Isaiah and Paul's letter to the Romans for the rest of the season.

These special days should have distinctive readings: Christmas Day (December 25): *Isaiah 11:1–10;* New Year's Day (January 1): *Hebrews 2:9–17;*

Epiphany: *Isaiah 60:1–6;* Baptism of the Lord: *Isaiah 61:1–11* or *John 1:19–34;* Presentation of the Lord (February 2): *Malachi 3:1–7.*

WINTER ORDINARY TIME

From February 3 until Ash Wednesday, read other letters of Saint Paul in their New Testament order: First and Second Corinthians, Galatians, Ephesians, Philippians, Colossians and Thessalonians.

LENT AND THE PASCHAL TRIDUUM

On Ash Wednesday read *Isaiah 58: 1–14* or *Joel 2:12– 17.* During the season (from Ash Wednesday to Holy Thursday night) read through Exodus and Jeremiah, Mark's gospel and the letter to the Hebrews.

On Palm Sunday the church reads the passion narratives from the gospels of Matthew (chapters 21– 27), Mark (chapters 11–15) or Luke (chapters 22–23). These would be fruitful passages for morning and evening prayer during the next several days. On Holy Thursday and Good Friday, the last supper and pas- sion stories from John (chapters 11–19) are appropri- ate, and on Holy Saturday choose from *Genesis 5:32— 8:22, Ezekiel 37: 1–14, Jonah 3:1–10, Daniel 3:1–24* and *Jeremiah 31:31–34.*

EASTER SEASON

During these 50 days, begin with the resurrection narratives in Matthew, chapter 28; Mark, chapter 16; Luke, chapter 24; and John, chapters 20–21. The Acts of the Apostles and Saint Peter's first letter will extend the story of the resurrection and its consequences. Also appropriate during the season is the entire gospel of John.

SUMMER AND FALL ORDINARY TIME

This long stretch of time from Pentecost to Advent provides an opportunity for continuous reading of particular sections. You could focus on one or more of the four gospels in succession (without the infancy and passion narratives) or the remaining New Testament letters of Paul, James, Peter, John and Jude. Sustained reading of any of the following Old Testament books would be fruitful: Genesis, 1 and 2 Samuel, 1 and 2 Kings, Ezra, Nehemiah, Esther, Judith and Ruth, Ezekiel, Daniel, and the minor prophets.

Hymns for Morning and Evening Prayer

ABOUT THESE HYMNS

Brother Aelred-Seton Shanley, a lay Benedictine monk, composed these beautiful hymns for morning and evening prayer. They are all long meter pieces (four-line stanzas, each line eight syllables) that may be recited as poetry or sung to these familiar hymn tunes:

Old hundredth
> All people that on earth do dwell
> Praise God from whom all blessings flow

Erhalt uns herr
> Again we keep this solemn fast
> Lord, keep us steadfast in thy word

Puer nobis
> What star is this with beams so bright?

Emmanuel (without refrain)
> O come, O come, Emmanuel

Tallis canon
> All praise to thee, my God, this night

SATURDAY EVENING

O fire that fuels the stars and suns,
rekindled in our evening flame:
your blinding radiance yet is dimmed
before the One from whom you came.

When out of darkness first you dawned,
you ushered in God's gifts untold:
on this the eighth, unequaled day,
you blazed where Life lay dead and cold.

For Christ, our light, unquenchable,
death sought to master and defy,
yet from a darkened, empty tomb
Life gave definitive reply.

The universe will not be shamed,
delighting God in endless ways,
for neither human sin nor pride
can silence its unceasing praise. Amen.

SUNDAY MORNING

First uttered, first conceived and named
by Love unbounded, unrestrained:
before all else that came to be,
"Light!" dark and silence overcame.

Without this nothing could endure,
yet through it, all life came to be!
Light's energies by God unleashed
would birth each world and galaxy.

Alone, apt symbol for the One
beyond all image and all form:
pervading all, yet uncontained,
of all that God has made, first born.

The fire within the burning bush,
the radiance seen on Moses' face,
the guide that led the magi forth,
Mount Tabor's brilliant, dazzling grace!

"Light!" pulse of everything alive,
from rainbow to the sun's fierce rays,
from fireflies to the farthest star,
you manifest God's hidden ways! Amen.

SUNDAY EVENING

Can we conceive when time was not,
the nothingness of cosmic sleep?
When, formless, there was only void:
no near, no far, no height, no deep?

In love's embrace, God's uttered Word
then sounded from Life's boundless heart:
like suns exploding into space,
"Light!" burst forth, dazzling, in the dark.

Upon the deep there spread delight
for God had smiled, and deemed it "good!"
Like solar winds was Wisdom's breath,
her warmth yet gentle on her brood.

Dividing light from darkness, then
God called light "Day!" and darkness "Night!"
Thus ev'ning came and morning came—
this first of days and God's delight. Amen.

MONDAY MORNING

Dawn's radiance washes over earth,
refreshed and rested from the night:
the grateful world, awake, aware
is bathed in Christ's baptismal light.

Emblazoned thus, our earth proclaims
its first foundation and its end.
Another day stirs life afresh:
its gifts from God to God all tend.

O Christ, indwelling source of life,
reflecting fair your Abba's face,
your radiance brightens all the earth
as we awake in your embrace.

Within your love we sing our praise,
transcendent God who nurture all;
day's dawning splendor sends us forth
to answer with our lives your call. Amen.

MONDAY EVENING

The blazing energies of light,
unleashed when God said "Let it be,"
in fusion formed the womb of life,
the rain clouds and the raging sea.

These parted, each to its domain,
divided by the vault of sky;
untamed and turbulent, unchecked,
within them life and death would vie.

Those waters clothed our planet home,
so terrible and yet so fair:
the gift without which all would cease,
yet placed, so fragile, in our care.

Both sign and sacrament of life,
of love awash, poured out and fresh:
engulfing all that sin would spawn,
while nurt'ring life in all the rest.

Thus evening came and morning came
that second day when waters burst:
both flood and freshness for our world,
chaste herald of our second birth. Amen.

TUESDAY MORNING

O sister dawn, how light your touch;
how bright your face upon the earth!
Awakened are we all to life
as you call us from sleep's small death.

You, sister, graced that Easter morn
when Life, entombed, was lost from sight.
You roused the women with their spice
and guided them to greet the Light!

Your dawning opens wide our eyes;
our talents are awakened, too!
Our hands, so grasping, rest has freed
to welcome gifts we never knew.

Aroused, awakened and aware,
hands turn to labor, hearts to pray:
what yesterday was only glimpsed
stands now as fresh and clear as day.

With dawn and all the gifts of day,
we praise you, Abba, Breath and Word:
a world so prodigal and free
reveals your loving hand, O God! Amen.

TUESDAY EVENING

Life, never bounded or constrained,
tamed chaos, took the floods in hand,
determined these should now recede
and bare what would become the land.

And so, this day, their bound'ries set,
God named one "Earth!" the other "Sea!"
And then, beholding both were good,
Love's eye was drawn to shrub and tree.

Life thus addressed our mother earth,
and charged her: Color, bloom and root!
Be lavish in the gifts you bear
of greening forests, plants and fruit!

And so it was and it was good!
Our planet's splendors stood untrod;
each peak, each valley, plain and pond
poured forth its poetry to God.

Thus evening came and morning came
the third day, when our earth first breathed;
so fragile, faithful, fruitful, free:
by Life sustained, by Love conceived! Amen.

WEDNESDAY MORNING

Where stretch the limits of the stars?
Who fathoms all the gifts of earth?
Within the origins of life
one Word, in labor, gives them birth.

Its silence fills the stellar night;
its sound plumbs deep our planet's core:
poured out for us, enfleshed in full,
this Word—none other—Mary bore.

From earth, the Word drew nourishment,
from us, the body we possess;
our sun provided warmth and light—
with these the Word took on our flesh.

All things created, great and small,
at dawn of time God sanctified:
now these, enfleshed within the Word,
return God's love, thus glorified.

For only thus the Word prepared
to consummate the sacrifice
for which God's heart had ever yearned,
for which Love would alone suffice.

Creation's dawning God deemed "Good!"
yet still we scarce believe our worth:
but pregnant, full, the Word here dawns,
and yearns in us to come to birth. Amen.

WEDNESDAY EVENING

There was no sun to rule the day,
no moon to roam the night until
our God flung forth the nebulae,
the planets, suns and stars at will.

With these God made the greater light
to dawn and blaze upon our day;
a lesser lamp illumined night
and marked each month along its way.

Thus time, the seasons and the years
began their endless ordered round;
the moon called forth the festivals
on which God's praises would resound.

And so it was and it was good!
Companions, friends, the stars would be:
bright beacons in the cosmic night,
sure bearings both on land and sea.

Thus evening came and morning came.
The fourth day saw our day-star, sun,
bright symbol of undying light,
undimmed when day and night are done. Amen.

THURSDAY MORNING

God's glory, Christ, our new-dawned day,
in deep compassion for our earth,
has raised what we had left for dead,
and healed what sin had scarred at birth.

The Alpha and Omega, Christ,
today and yesterday: the same!
who manifests the great unseen:
who by the nameless One is named!

Word of God's silence, sounding still
beneath the surface of each day;
both cloud by day and flame by night,
companion, goal, our guide and way.

We bless you, Abba, brimming love,
and Christ, your well-beloved Son,
who with your Spirit breathe in us:
three-personed yet for ever one. Amen.

THURSDAY EVENING

Our mother earth, her mantle green,
lay ripened, seeded and at rest;
she yearned to nurture all to life,
providing nourishment and nest.

So God, unbounded, uncontained,
ordained the oceans teem with life
and bid the skies be filled with flight:
with fish and fowl the world was rife.

These each were blest and both deemed good!
God urged them mate and multiply:
thus life would ever be increased
and God in all be glorified.

With song and plumage, soaring flight,
birds blazoned forth God's gifts so free;
while sea-life, fathomless and feared,
reflected, dark, God's mystery.

Thus evening came and morning came
the fifth day, filling air and sea.
Life overflowing and outpoured
depends upon diversity! Amen.

FRIDAY MORNING

Lord, lover of the human heart,
earth's source, her dawn, her day and rest:
how holy is our planet-home,
whose gifts your love all manifest.

So deep your love, so reckless, sure,
you loved us even in our sin:
pursued us, shared our pain and death,
determined at the last to win!

Embrace, enfold us in your breath;
so warmed, may we be set ablaze.
Close draw us to your wounded side—
the wounds we bear will then be grace.

Love, crucified, twice hallows earth,
which God deemed good and filled with grace:
here, holy ground; here, heaven's gate;
with awe therefore our earth embrace!

We bless you, holy, deathless One!
We bless you, Christ, God's wounded Word!
We bless you, Breath, our breath and life;
your praise through all the earth be heard!
    Amen.

FRIDAY EVENING

The fields and plains were still ungrazed,
the ground untouched by things that crawl,
when God called creatures forth to play,
and wondrously earth bore them all.

Then Life, beholding all was good,
in overflowing joy conceived:
"Let us now human beings make!"
God gave them breath that Sabbath eve.

"Let them, together and alone,
our image be, our likeness bear.
To you I give your kin the beasts
and all the earth into your care.

"For she has borne all living things;
her fruits will give you nourishment.
As for the flocks and herds, let them
with grass and foliage be content."

Thus evening came and morning came,
the sixth day, giving God delight,
for everything was very good,
one with another ordered right!

The earth, God saw, was now complete—
a marvel of diversity!
So mirrors earth its Maker's life,
revealed within the Trinity. Amen.

SATURDAY MORNING

Creator of this dawning day,
creation finds its rest in you:
though all must change and taste decay,
you touch our hearts and they are new!

We bless you, Abba, for this earth,
for all the wonder it retains.
Though we may spurn you in our sin,
your selfless gift of love remains.

Touched by this gift may mind and heart
your praise throughout the world proclaim,
and may this love deep in our hearts
set others blazing with its flame.

The seventh day, this day of rest,
you call us to rehearse your reign:
to cease from work and with delight
to rev'rence all that you sustain.

Most blessed Trinity of love,
for whom the human heart was made,
to you be praise in ceaseless song
on this our Sabbath, blessed day! Amen.

BASIC PRAYERS

ABOUT PRAYER

For Christians, prayer is partly learned and partly received as a gift from God. We learn to pray by using normal human efforts to repeat the consecrated texts of our tradition. With persistent use, these verbal forms of prayer support and enrich our personal ways of speaking to God from our hearts.

But prayer is also a gift. In the sacraments of Christian initiation the Holy Spirit is poured out in our hearts and there cries to God continuously, "Abba, dear Father" (Galatians 4:6). The Spirit praying within us is an irresistible impulse toward God, although we can become dull to its promptings.

We have the very breath of God pulsating in us, urging us toward the invisible Presence. We have also received a set of basic prayers to memorize and use every day as channels for the Spirit's power: the Sign of the Cross, the Apostles' Creed, the Lord's Prayer, the Hail Mary, the doxologies and others. Along with the psalms and canticles of the Bible, these are gifts of the Spirit coming to us through our church's tradition. By way of parents, catechists and friends, our faith community hands over these prayers to us, sometimes orally, sometimes through books.

THE SIGN OF THE CROSS

The church imposes on us this essential sign in baptism and confirmation and we use it in many ways: to sign our lips to open them in praise; to sign our forehead, lips and heart at the reading of the gospel; to sign our children on their foreheads at bedtime; to sign our whole body, from head to heart and from left to right shoulder, as a shield of faith and an act of commitment and rededication to Christ. As we begin morning and evening prayer, we make the sign of the cross on our lips, often with the words, "O Lord, open my lips . . ." We use the full sign of the cross at the end of these hours and also when beginning the gospel canticles of Zachary (at morning prayer), Mary (at evening prayer) and Simeon (at night prayer). When the sign of the cross is used on other occasions, the words are always these:

In the name + of the Father,
and of the Son,
and of the Holy Spirit. Amen.

THE APOSTLES' CREED

This basic profession of the Christian faith is given to us in baptism. It originated in the profession of faith that was made at Rome as new Christians were immersed three times in the baptismal pool in the name of the three persons of the Trinity. Through the Creed, we renew our baptismal vows committing us to Christ and his gospel.

I believe in God, the Father almighty,
    creator of heaven and earth.

I believe in Jesus Christ, God's only Son, our Lord,
    who was conceived by the Holy Spirit,
    born of the Virgin Mary,
    suffered under Pontius Pilate,
    was crucified, died, and was buried;
    he descended to the dead.
    On the third day he rose again;
    he ascended into heaven,
    he is seated at the right hand of the Father,
    and he will come to judge the living and the dead.

I believe in the Holy Spirit,
    the holy catholic church,
    the communion of saints,
    the forgiveness of sins,
    the resurrection of the body,
    and the life everlasting. Amen.

THE LORD'S PRAYER

Often called simply the "Our Father," this prayer, too, is a gift of the Holy Spirit praying in us. The Lord Jesus himself taught it to his first disciples (Matthew 6:9–13, Luke 11:1–4), and the church put it on our lips in baptism and authorized and empowered us to say it as children of God. The earliest recorded instance of its use is in the Didache, *a late-first-century document that tells us to say the Lord's Prayer three times a day. This beautiful prayer gives us words to pray and also a model for all of our prayers. It shows us how to pray and what to pray for.*

OLDER VERSION

Our Father, who art in heaven,
    hallowed be thy name;
    thy kingdom come;
    thy will be done on earth as it is in heaven.
Give us this day our daily bread;
    and forgive us our trespasses
    as we forgive those who trespass against us;
    and lead us not into temptation,
    but deliver us from evil.

For the kingdom, the power, and the glory are yours,
    now and for ever. Amen.

MODERN VERSION

Our Father in heaven,
    hallowed be your name,
    your kingdom come,
    your will be done, on earth as in heaven.
Give us today our daily bread.

Forgive us our sins
   as we forgive those who sin against us.
Save us from the time of trial
   and deliver us from evil.

For the kingdom, the power, and the glory are yours,
   now and for ever. Amen.

HAIL MARY

The Hail Mary is a combination of two texts in the gospel of Luke (1:26–45). In the first part the Archangel Gabriel salutes the Virgin Mary (verse 28) and in the second part her cousin Elizabeth, the mother of John the Baptist, moved by the Holy Spirit, hails her as doubly blessed (verse 42). The third part of the Hail Mary was developed in the late Middle Ages.

Hail, Mary, full of grace, the Lord is with you.
Blessed are you among women,
   and blessed is the fruit of your womb, Jesus.
Holy Mary, Mother of God, pray for us sinners,
   now and at the hour of our death. Amen.

DOXOLOGIES

Doxologies are the church's most fundamental and widely used acts of praise to the Blessed Trinity. The greater doxology (Gloria in excelsis Deo) is used at Mass and the lesser ones in the Liturgy of the Hours, usually at the end of hymns, psalms and canticles. Just as the Sign of the Cross is accompanied by a physical signing of the body, so a doxology is used with a bow of the head and body to the Holy Trinity. The following are several forms of the doxology:

Glory to the Father, and to the Son,
and to the Holy Spirit:
as it was in the beginning, is now,
and will be for ever. Amen.

Glory to you, Source of all Being,
Eternal Word,
and Holy Spirit:
as it was in the beginning, is now,
and will be for ever. Amen.

Glory to God: Creator, Redeemer, and Sanctifier,
now and always and for ever and ever. Amen.

To the King of the ages, immortal, invisible,
the only wise God,
be honor and glory, through Jesus Christ,
for ever and ever. Amen.

THE THREE GOSPEL CANTICLES

These three canticles appear in Luke's gospel, sung by three important figures in the story of the incarnation of the Word of God: Zachary, the father of John the Baptist; Mary, the mother of Jesus; and Simeon, the prophet. They are revered in the Eastern and Western liturgies, especially at morning, evening and night prayer.

CANTICLE OF ZACHARY *Luke 1:68–79*

Blessed are you, + Lord, the God of Israel,
you have come to your people and set them free.
You have raised up for us a mighty Savior,
born of the house of your servant David.
Through your holy prophets, you promised
    of old
to save us from our enemies,
from the hands of all who hate us,
to show mercy to our forebears,
and to remember your holy covenant.
This was the oath you swore
    to our father Abraham:
to set us free from the hands of our enemies,
free to worship you without fear,
holy and righteous before you,
all the days of our life.

And you, child, shall be called the prophet
    of the Most High,
for you will go before the Lord to prepare
    the way,
to give God's people knowledge of salvation
by the forgiveness of their sins.
In the tender compassion of our God
the dawn from on high shall break upon us,
to shine on those who dwell in darkness
    and the shadow of death,
and to guide our feet into the way of peace.

CANTICLE OF MARY *Luke 1:46–55*

My soul ✝ proclaims the greatness of the Lord,
my spirit rejoices in God my Savior,
for you, Lord, have looked with favor on your
    lowly servant.

From this day all generations will call me
    blessed:
you, the Almighty, have done great things for me
and holy is your name.
You have mercy on those who fear you,
from generation to generation.

You have shown strength with your arm
and scattered the proud in their conceit,
casting down the mighty from their thrones
and lifting up the lowly.
You have filled the hungry with good things
and sent the rich away empty.

You have come to the aid of your servant Israel,
to remember the promise of mercy,
the promise made to our forebears,
to Abraham and his children for ever.

CANTICLE OF SIMEON *Luke 2:29–32*

Now, + Lord, you let your servant go in peace:
your word has been fulfilled.
My own eyes have seen the salvation
which you have prepared in the sight
   of every people:
a light to reveal you to the nations
and the glory of your people Israel.

THE JESUS PRAYER

One of the oldest, simplest and best of prayers is a calling in faith upon the Holy Name of Jesus. By repeatedly invoking the proper name of our Savior, chosen by God and given to Mary and Joseph by the angel Gabriel, Christians are convinced that they will be enabled to penetrate more and more deeply and surely into a growing awareness of the presence of God who saves and sanctifies us from within.

   The Holy Name is sometimes repeated by itself and sometimes in a phrase. The most common form of the fuller invocation is:

Lord Jesus Christ, Son of the living God,
have mercy on me, a sinner.

   The best way to say the Jesus Prayer is to sit in as much physical and inner stillness as one can manage and then repeat the invocation over and over, slowly and steadily, fixing the mind directly and intensely on the words of the prayer itself, without trying to conjure up any mental pictures or intellectual concepts. One should pray in this way without strain but with real effort for some length of time at each attempt. Rosary beads are a useful timer and reminder in this effort.

Persistent, frequent attempts to pray in this way will gradually habituate the soul to more effortless and continuous use of the Holy Name until it becomes the very substance of one's life of prayer. It is well to use the Jesus Prayer before and after other forms of prayer, such as the forms of morning and evening prayer contained in this prayer book. It can also be used during normal intervals in the day's work, when walking from place to place, for example, even when conditions are not ideal for recollected kinds of prayer.

Great saints and fervent mystics of both East and West tell us that the Jesus Prayer can even become self-acting as it descends from the lips and mind into the heart, the very center of our being. Such a gift is, of course, a pure grace, but it can be prepared for, in the first place, by genuine effort in a spirit of faith.

The Jesus Prayer is a high act of faith and self-surrender to the indwelling Spirit who longs to teach us to pray without ceasing to Abba, our dear and heavenly Father. It is a sure path to contemplative prayer and to "the peace that passes all understanding" (Philippians 4:7).

Acknowledgments continued from page iv

Passages from the Psalms are from *The Psalms: Grail Translation from the Hebrew* © 1993 by Ladies of the Grail (England). Used by permission of GIA Publications, Inc., exclusive agent. All rights reserved.

The following passages of scripture are from The Revised Common Lectionary in *Readings for the Assembly,* New Revised Standard Version, Emended. Minneapolis: Augsburg Fortress, 1997: pp. 30, 34, 48, 82, 116–17, 157–58, 172, 172–73, 220–21, 223 and 232.

The scripture reading on p. 77 is from the *Revised English Bible* in The Complete Parallel Bible. New York: Oxford University Press, 1993.

All other passages of scripture are from the *New Revised Standard Version of the Bible* © 1989 Division of Christian Education of the National Council for the Churches of Christ in the United States of America. All rights reserved.

Canticles on pages 53–54, 145–46 and 154–55 are from *Today's English Version of the Bible,* in *Good News Bible.* New York: American Bible Society. 1976, 1979.

Canticles on pages 31, 49, 62, 82–83, 211–12, 241 and 246 are from *The New Zealand Prayer Book.* Aukland: Collins, 1989.

The Canticle of Zachary and Canticle of Mary on pages 13–14, 73–74, 77–78, 141 and 206–7 are by Owen Alstott, © 1991 and © 1993 respectively, published by Oregon Catholic Press in *Today's Missal: Music Edition* 1999, numbers 488 and 684.

The Canticle of Zachary on page 202 is by Ruth Duck from *Gather Comprehensive.* Chicago: GIA, 1994.

The following items are taken from *Praying Together,* English Language Liturgical Consultation, Abingdon Press: 1988: The Canticle of the Church on pages 9–10 and 137–38, as well as parts of it used as intercessions on pp. 14 and 142, the Apostles' Creed on page 287, the modern version of the Lord's Prayer on pp. 288–89, and the Canticle of Zachary, Canticle of Mary and Canticle of Simeon on pp. 291, 292 and 293.

Prayers, canticles and intercessions on pages 40, 41, 67–68, 192, 196–97 and 207–8 are from *The Book of Common Prayer* according to the use of The Episcopal Church. New York: The Church Hymnal Corporation and Seabury Press, 1977.

The antiphon on p. 77 is from *A Book of Prayers*. Washington, D.C.: International Commission on English in the Liturgy: 1982.

The Canticle of Praise of St. Francis of Assisi on pages 176–77 and the closing prayer on p. 178 are from Regis Armstrong and Ignatius Brady, *Francis and Clare: The Complete Works*. Mahwah, New Jersey: Paulist Press, 1988.

The doxology "Glory to you . . ." is from *The New Companion to the Breviary*, Carmelites of Indianapolis, 1988.

God should be adored, p. 1: *On Prayer*, chapter 35.

Let us stand, p. 64: *The Rule of St. Benedict*, chapter 19:7 in *RB1980, The Rule of St. Benedict in Latin and English with Notes*, ed. Timothy Fry. Collegeville: Liturgical Press, 1981, p. 216.

The scriptures lie ever, p. 128: *Conferences*, Conference 10, trans. Colm Luibheid. New York: Paulist Press, 1985, p. 137.

Prayer is the key, p. 193: *The Mind of Mahatma Gandhi*, eds. R. K. Prabhu, and U. R. Rao. Ahmedabad: Navajivan Publishing, 1968, p. 87.

You move us, p. 266: *The Confessions*, Book I:i.